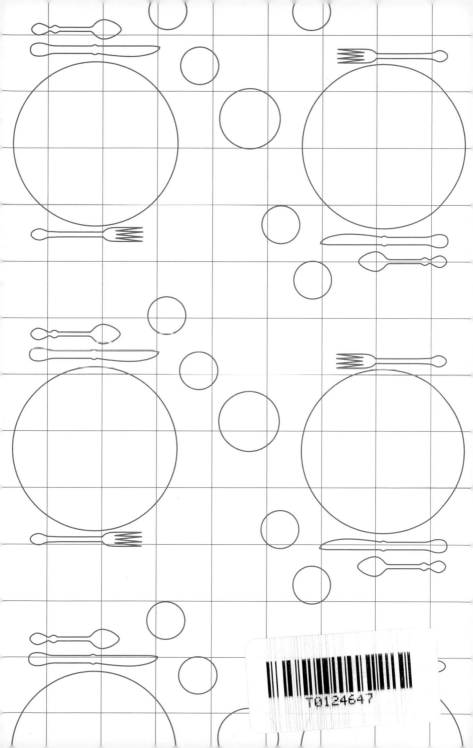

HOW TO HOST
A DINNER PARTY

HOW TO HOST
A DINNER PARTY

COREY MINTZ

Illustrations by Steve Murray

ANANSI

This edition published in 2013 by
House of Anansi Press Inc.
houseofanansi.com

House of Anansi Press is committed to protecting our natural environment.
This book is made of material from well-managed FSC®-certified forests,
recycled materials, and other controlled sources.

House of Anansi Press is a Global Certified Accessible™ (GCA by Benetech)
publisher. The ebook version of this book meets stringent accessibility
standards and is available to readers with print disabilities.

27 26 25 24 23   2 3 4 5 6

Library and Archives Canada Cataloguing in Publication

Mintz, Corey, 1975-
How to host a dinner party / Corey Mintz ; Steve Murray,
illustrator.
Issued also in electronic format.
ISBN 978-1-77089-230-9
1. Entertaining. 2. Dinners and dining. I. Title.
BJ2038.M56 2013   395.3   C2012-906739-3

Library of Congress Control Number: 2012950668

Cover design: Steve Murray
Text design and typesetting: Alysia Shewchuk

*House of Anansi Press is grateful for the privilege to work on and create from the
Traditional Territory of many Nations, including the Anishinabeg, the Wendat, and
the Haudenosaunee, as well as the Treaty Lands of the Mississaugas of the Credit.*

 Canada Council   Conseil des Arts
for the Arts   du Canada

 ONTARIO ARTS COUNCIL
CONSEIL DES ARTS DE L'ONTARIO

*We acknowledge for their financial support of our publishing program
the Canada Council for the Arts, the Ontario Arts Council, and the Government of
Canada through the Canada Book Fund.*

Printed and bound in China

For my father, the astronaut,
and my mother, the senator.

CONTENTS

INTRODUCTION

by Sarah Polley

ONCE HAD A DRIVING INSTRUCTOR WHO TAUGHT IN a way that made every lesson a life lesson. He had a knack for turning the specifics of driving into universal wisdom. One day, as we were driving on a busy Toronto street, I heard a car horn honk and yelped, "What did I do?"

"That honk wasn't for you," he said softly. "You are at a point where you worry too much about what other drivers think about you. You may reach a point where you don't worry enough. Try to find a balance."

For me, the only thing that has replicated the experience of learning so much about life from studying a specific skill is the reading of this book. It teaches you how to create a beautiful experience for the people you care about in the context of a dinner party. But since reading it I find myself applying many of the lessons in this book to my relationships and life in general. Be prepared. Be thoughtful. Listen. Watch for clues on how people are feeling and do what you can to make them feel comfortable, taken care of, and well fed!

I first knew Corey Mintz as a teenager, when his idea of cooking came from the back page of our copy of the *New Basics Cookbook*. The spine of the book was unbroken. On the very last page, in coloured marker, was written "Call Garlic Pepper on Yonge Street. Get them to bring food." It was our only recipe and we used it every night that we didn't eat Alphagetti. Corey and I lived with each other as delinquent teenagers. When I was fifteen I had major spinal surgery and Corey found himself caring for a child while he was still a child himself. He took care of me. Better care than a nurse or relative could have. He learned to cook. I remember lying in bed and hearing the clattering of utensils as he struggled his way through recipes, and the beautiful smells coming from the kitchen as he proudly completed a meal. Corey was and is an eccentric, sometimes brittle person who is capable of great tenderness. Through learning to cook, he developed an eloquent, uncomplicated way of showing love without irony.

Corey now hosts dinner parties for a living. For years he has had a weekly column called FED in the *Toronto Star*, centered around a dinner party he hosts for an interesting, eclectic group of people. I usually read with envy at his lucky guests who sometimes walk in without knowing what a treat they are in for. I've heard at least two FED guests say later that it was the best night of their year.

Recently Corey invited me over for dinner because it had been awhile and, as he said, "I've learned a lot about hosting since the last time you were here." He wasn't lying. Every dinner party experience I've had in the last ten years at Corey's has been incredible. But practice really does make perfect and I can now honestly say there is nowhere I'd rather be in the world than at his table. The food is always stunning, but that's not what I remember or what is important. What stays with me is the atmosphere he creates, the table and the people around it, and the feeling of being seamlessly taken care and thought of without ever feeling it happen. Somehow joy always arrives at his table, without him seeming to do anything specific to invite it.

It's possible to leave these gatherings intimidated. There is such a frightening organization and charm to the host that it makes you wonder if you should ever bother to attempt to replicate it at your own home. Even though the night is seemingly perfect, Corey himself always seems to be having a good time. He always seems relaxed, engaged and the night appears effortless for him. I can't begin to express the relief I felt in reading this book and realizing there was a method to his success. What I love most about this book is the way it illustrates that your experience and your guests' experiences are intertwined. This is a guide to creating the maximum joy for your guests with minimum stress to yourself. Since you set the tone for the evening, it is paramount that you feel good about it. After reading the book I found it was possible to go back over the dinner parties I'd attended or hosted in my mind to figure out what went wrong, what could have been done differently, and how to avoid those pitfalls in the future. Moreover, it made me feel excited to host more dinner parties of my own.

Corey, it turns out, is a skilled alchemist and he is generous enough to share his formulas. This book is a detailed anthropological study of what makes a great social experience over food, combined with a practical how-to manual to create what could be some of the most rewarding nights of your life.

When you leave a place with Corey, whether it be a party, a movie theater, or a shopping trip, it's always somewhat frightening how he breaks down, analyzes and picks apart what an experience was for him and why. (It was especially unpleasant after he read my last script and left no detail of his utter disdain unarticulated.) He has a ruthless, unblinking eye — which is incredibly helpful in book form. Like the man himself, this book is fun, engaging, hilarious, brutally honest, chock full of truths you don't want to hear but should probably listen to, infuriating, and always entertaining.

You may feel you don't need this advice on how to host a dinner party. Maybe you don't. But I guarantee your guests will have a better time if you listen to it. Corey has the key to something ephemeral. He has broken it down and made something mysterious readable. Where we mortals see a mess of food and conversation, Corey sees a glowing map, a series of manageable steps — a recipe.

I hope you host more dinner parties. I hope this book makes you more excited, confident, and less afraid to do so. I know I myself feel much more assured in my ability to throw a great one after reading it. If more people gathered in environments where they were in great company, well fed, and well cared for, the world would be a much happier place.

PROLOGUE

FIFTEEN MINUTES BEFORE THE ARRIVAL OF RUTH
Reichl, on a cool spring day, I was sweating. Never
before or since have I been as nervous as a cook,
host, or interviewer. The butterflies in my stomach had
butterflies in their stomachs.

At the time I was a restaurant critic for the *Toronto Star*,
and Reichl was the editor of *Gourmet*. Before that she'd
been the restaurant critic for the *New York Times* and the
L.A. Times. Her third autobiographical book, *Garlic and
Sapphires*, an account of how she disguised her identity
to go undetected in New York's best restaurants, had an
influence on me and probably every food writer in North
America that cannot be overestimated.

Why did I think it was a good idea to serve her lunch?

Just two years earlier I'd been a cook, desperate to transition out of a career I was painfully unqualified for. And that's not my stab at false modesty. In any field, you can look around the room and tell who has the talent or drive to succeed above others, and who is treading water. I worked with some inspiring, tireless chefs, the type of men and women who would climb to the top of that particular mountain. I recognized that I didn't have what they had.

One night when I was hosting dinner, my friend Lily Cho brought me Reichl's book *Tender to the Bone* instead of a bottle of wine. At the end of that evening, Lily and her then-boyfriend Jesse Brown suggested that I should become a professional dinner party host. It was the sort of sweet but unhelpful advice a child might offer, like suggesting that I should become a candy taster or a hoverbike repairman.

I chugged back Reichl's book, and then the next one and the next one. Beyond the flash of her spy-game disguises, what made an impression was the consideration that went into each review, the burden she expressed over judging strangers in such a public forum. I remember thinking that if I ever got to do that job, I would do it like her.

In an unlikely plot twist, I did get to do that job. And two years later, my hero's publicist was asking me if I wanted to interview Reichl, who had a new book coming out. In situations like this, you get about thirty to sixty minutes with the interview subject, usually in a hotel room, with a queue of other newspaper writers waiting their turn. When it's a food personality, you're expected to drag them to your favourite restaurant or café, as if they weren't exhausted with the triteness of being used as a prop.

Everyone had a suggestion about where to take Reichl for lunch, the soundness of trying to impress her with opulence weighed against the street cred of showing her some dingy Chinatown hole. Lily told me I should make lunch for Reichl. It was a fantastic idea — and it terrified me. Reichl was like Batman, and I was the kid with the towel tied around his neck to look like a cape. Frightened enough of interviewing a living legend, I didn't need to add cooking performance anxiety.

But I put myself in my guest's shoes. As a restaurant critic you're not allowed to complain about your work because it is the best job ever. But what most people don't know is that most restaurants are terrible and eating expensive, rich food gets tiring. Often you just want a simple sandwich.

So I made us GLT (guanciale, lettuce, and tomato) sandwiches. This was a valuable lesson for later. When you really need to impress someone, choose the simplest thing and make it well.

Reichl turned out to be everything I'd hoped: gracious, thoughtful (she walked over and joined me at the counter as I assembled our sandwiches), funny, and candid. She helped make it feel less like an interview and more like two old friends having lunch, asking where I'd gotten the bread, the guanciale, where the tomatoes were grown, if I'd made my own aioli (phew, I had).

Since I was on deadline, the interview was turned around quickly. But once I was done with it I still had that performance high, so I wrote a blog post about how it felt to cook for my idol. Six months later my boss called me into her office.

"Remember the interview you did with Ruth Reichl?" she asked. "I'm not saying it wasn't good." I didn't like where this was going.

"But the blog post you wrote," she continued, "about what you'd cooked and why was better." She had an idea. "Do you think you could do that every week?"

And that's how I became a professional dinner party host.

If reviewing restaurants for a living had taught me one thing, it's that you should eat at home. I adore restaurants. But the good ones are few. And the most transcendent experiences, the dazzle of brilliant food, the pampering of efficient service will never trump the joyful intimacy of the dinner party.

No matter how much we drink at home, we will never face the sticker shock of a bill. We can be as loud as we wish. There is no one waiting at the door, hungrily, for our table.

Having cooked for six years and having hosted many successful dinner parties, I thought I knew what I was doing. But I didn't. Like most people, I figured that a dinner party was a matter of inviting a bunch of people and serving them food. The intricacies of social balance, the smoothness of service, were beyond my thinking at the time. The guests, I figured, could sort that out.

When I'd interviewed Reichl, I hadn't even thought to bring her a glass of water until she asked for one — such an obvious thing.

In the beginning, I invited guests who were completely

incompatible. I tried to impress people. I asked for feedback at the table. It was a year before I bought wineglasses or matching plates. It was two years until I bought cloth napkins or a proper dining-room table. But week by week, with the mandate to interview guests over dinner, I kept building on what I'd learned. I discovered the subtleties of what people needed from me as a host. I figured out what space I had to experiment, and where and when in the meal I needed a proven hit.

Every week was someone and something new. It may seem Nixonian, but for the purpose of writing my column, I've recorded every one of these dinners. In listening to and transcribing these conversations — with politicians, artists, academics, monkeys, librarians, chefs, fishmongers, butchers, competitive barbecuers, dogwalkers, sommeliers, cops, lawyers, psychologists, writers, activists, a spy, two alleged terrorists, a forager, a rabbi, an acupuncturist, a high-rise window washer, a comic book talent scout, an economist, a drug addict, a mayor, and a world poker champion — I am able to hear what went right or wrong at the dinner table, and make notes for improvement.

I learned that the golden rule for dinner parties supersedes the original golden rule.

As tempting as it is to be sidetracked by the soufflé that didn't rise, the person who came thirty minutes late, the passive-aggressive text from your intern, or the corked bottle of Pinot Noir, those are all distractions. Your goal is to ensure that your guests enjoy themselves — not that they be impressed by your cooking or envious of your home.

Every dinner, every guest, is different, requiring and deserving of thoughtful attention. Our task is to make them comfortable. This is why we take their coat, get them a drink, introduce them to new people, inquire about their work, their family, their renovations. But the familiarity, the mundane predictability of these topics, should usher us to move as quickly as possible past work, the weather, vacation plans. Dinner has struck gold when guests can argue respect-fully about politics and race while still reaching for one last spoonful of cassoulet. Most guests, even those who seemed like they came only to appease their spouse (and these are the worst guests of all, as we shall discuss in Chapter One), will eventually relax. You can see this in their posture, the openness of their dialogue. It can happen in five minutes or an hour. Our challenge as hosts, and our talent, if we can find it, is to shorten this time frame.

Contrary to popular belief, you don't need to spend a lot of money on a dinner party. And you don't need to be a great cook either. What you need to be is a great friend and a better planner.

Not long ago I found myself in Lily's home, this time with her husband, Zach. They'd just hosted a dinner party and had asked me to stay for a late-night drink. These are people with a lot of education and accomplish-ments between them, strong cooking skills, and no lack of thoughtfulness. And yet they had pre-plated the salads a half-hour before anyone sat down. When they'd asked me if that was a bad idea, I started to explain what I thought was relatively common sense — that an acidic salad dress-ing starts to corrode lettuce as soon as it makes contact, that assembling a salad is to be done at the absolute last minute. When they asked if I had any other tips, I started talking and found twenty minutes had gone by, with still more to say, when Lily interjected to tell me, in a maternal tone, that I needed to write a book.

She was right. After you've hosted more than 150 dinner parties, after you've done anything that many times, much of it seems like common sense. But that's the deception of experience.

Most people would like to host a dinner party but are afraid. Or they have misplaced confidence and subject friends to their attempts at reproducing the complicated recipes of celebrity chefs. Worse, many have been led to believe, by television, that hosting is a competition.

This book aims to guide readers through everything they need to know about hosting, an experience that should be more fun and less stressful. It will explain why we like to gather for dinner, when we should host, whom we should invite, what we should cook, and how we should cook it in a way that doesn't make us cry.

Having organized what I've learned into ten chapters, I think you can become a great host without doing it as many times as I have. After all, you have the advantage of cooking only for friends rather than strangers.

If I could be anywhere, I wouldn't be lying on a beach or hiking through the rainforests. I would be at the dinner table with friends.

CHAPTER ONE

EVERY TERRIBLE DINNER PARTY BEGINS WITH A bad decision. Since forever ago, husbands and wives have looked up from their glossy magazines or iPads or sacred scrolls and said, "Honey, we should have so-and-so over for dinner," or "Honey, we should cook such-and-such for dinner." I have been the guest at many overcrowded, miscast, inedible dinner parties that began with these well-intentioned impulses. And so have you.

The shame of the human race is that we can put a robot on Mars, yet we can't figure out how to host a dinner party. But really, it's as easy when we take it one step at a time. Start by assessing your table.

THE TABLE

 Don't invite more guests than you can handle.

In a mad rush to announce their Moroccan/Thai/Star Wars–themed dinner, or as an opportunity to show off their new decanter, belt, or fiancé, too many hosts skip right over this first step. Once we've figured out the why of a dinner party, but before we ask whom we should invite or when, we've got to determine how many people we can accommodate.

Thinking of squeezing in one more invitation? Then visualize a tightly packed suitcase. Now try to find space for a bottle of wine. It might fit, but it might shatter and ruin everything.

We've all been at a dinner where we're strapped into our chairs like astronauts, unable to move an inch in either direction (which is acceptable only if it's a family holiday dinner). Or have you ever had a restaurant squeeze your party of eight into a six-person table? Remember how every time a dish arrived, the server didn't know where to put it down, and you all had to rearrange your glasses, plates, and cutlery?

So if we're in agreement that there is such a thing as too many people at the table, we can get realistic about defining that number. Go take a look at your table right now. Ask yourself how many people can sit at this table comfortably, with food and wine. And remember, if you're serving family style, those big bowls are going to take up major real estate. Want to have candles on the table? That eats up more space. How about a vase of flowers in the centre? That's a trick question. The centrepiece, whether it's flowers, a candelabra, or a diorama, is a stupid nuisance that only gets in the way.

Now that you've taken a serious look at your table, gather all your chairs around it and have a sit. If your chairs have arms, you're probably pretty cozy, like in a movie theatre. But those arms take an extra half a foot per chair and make it harder for guests to excuse themselves to go to the powder room. This is why we shop for thin, high-backed dining-room chairs. The average guest requires (and this should in no way be interpreted as canonical) about 26 in. (66 cm) of width. Though we're not all the same size, that's a reasonable average to follow.

The number that you've just determined is not elastic. This is how many guests you can invite. Want to invite more people? Get a bigger table. Can't fit in a bigger table? Get a bigger home. Can't afford a bigger home? Then start being reasonable. At least you have somewhere to sit. I was once asked, "Do I need a table?" Yes, you need a table.

But don't sweat perfection at this moment. When I started hosting, I was using plywood chairs that cost $10 at IKEA. They were so flimsy that one finally snapped under the weight of a jolly guest. When those were all broken, I found some plastic folding things on Craigslist. Only when I was ready did I start shopping for nice dining-room chairs.

We don't "need" nice things. We want them. But sometimes our insecurity about what is expected of us makes us feel that we must own certain items — not for their usefulness, but as status symbols. Nice chairs, like nice wineglasses, plates, cutlery, and candlesticks, are things we can acquire in good time.

My old table sat six, so for one hundred professional dinners, I only ever invited five guests. My new table is a big piece of reclaimed maple. It seats eight. A ninth person would limit everyone's elbow room and the space on the table. If guests are not comfortable, they cannot have a good time.

I was tempted, when shopping for this table, to buy one a foot longer, which could have accommodated ten guests. But beyond the limit of space in my home, it forced me to confront the question: How often do I want to have ten people over? Rarely to never.

There's nothing wrong with multiple conversations happening at once. In fact, it can be wonderful. Whether everyone is listening to one blowhard expounding or three separate discussions are occurring simultaneously, it's exciting to see people engaged. With groups of four and eight people, it is still possible to have a single conversation. Beyond that, the dialogue becomes fragmented, often balkanized. In this type of situation, you'll likely see people defecting from one side of the table to the other, voting with their feet on whether they want to talk about reproductive rights or the latest episode of that show with the pretty single girl who is great at her job but terrible at everything else.

However, once the head count reaches nine, it will be impossible to moderate. And a conversation is like a garden. Mostly you want to let it grow naturally. But every once in a while, you need to tie it to a stick before it reaches too far in the wrong direction. Also, once the table gets too large, there will be people at either end who don't get to say more than hello to each other. If the event extends to more than one table, it's no longer a dinner party. It's a banquet.

Just because you can seat many doesn't mean you have to. If you want a quiet, intimate evening, accept that your capacity is six. Know your limits before you start writing your invitation list.

THE DATE AND THE GUEST LIST

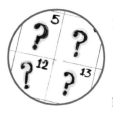

Beware the natural desire to crowd-source a date for your party. Democracy is a nice idea for government, but it is an aggravation for hosting dinner. Emailing six friends and asking them to propose a date that works for everyone may seem like a reasonable way to begin, but it's asking for trouble. Couple A responds right away, suggesting a date but without cc-ing the others. Couple B isn't available for the next six weekends. Couple C has a private beef with Couple A and are waiting to hear if they're coming, which is a deal-breaker.

That's why setting the date and choosing the guests are interchangeable, depending on your agenda. Do you want to set dinner on a designated evening and then see who is available? Or are there specific people you want to have over and whose schedules you're willing to work around?

In the date-first model, use a ranked ballot system for guests. So first you choose a date, say, three Saturdays from now. Then you contact your first pick of guests (probably a couple, probably your best friends). They can't make the 17th? Okay, how about the 24th? Once you've decided on

ON BANQUETS AND BUFFETS

 A potluck does count as a dinner party, but banquets and buffets do not.

A potluck is an alternate style of dinner party, in which each guest brings a dish. Other than its general horridness, there is nothing specifically wrong with a potluck. But the labour of organizing people to bring different things to avoid a collection of six bean dips is often more trouble than cooking yourself. Whether you have friends who are good cooks or bad, the democratization of labour removes the host's ability to author the evening. We have to endure either someone's terrible cabbage soup or the fact that he is pouting about its unpopularity.

Once we expand beyond a single table for a sit-down dinner, this is called a banquet. And while the word conjures images of regality, it detracts from the home dining experience. When I think of a banquet, it is not a seventeenth-century royal court. It is a wedding, an academic symposium, summer camp, a political trade conference, or some other situation where people are gathered, primarily not to eat, but they've been there long enough that they need to be either fed

or shot. I think of large rooms in suburban strip malls or in the basements of downtown hotels and convention centres. I feel the sting of uncomfortable rented chairs, the gnawing irritation of being served last out of thirty tables or the guilt of being served first. And never, in any of these venues, have I witnessed anything that remotely resembled a well-cooked meal (other than when a whole pig or goat was being roasted). If you were to sneak into the kitchen, where I have worked as a catering cook, you would see plates stacked as high as the boxes in Charles Foster Kane's warehouse. Pre-dressed with vegetables or sauces, each plate is crowned with a rubbery slab of chicken or fish scooped from a metal insert (where a pile of a hundred chicken breasts continue to steam each other) before a queue of servers grab the dishes, four at a time, to ferry them out to the wrong place settings.

As soon as you step beyond the reasonable boundary of one table, you are setting foot in this territory. One by one, you will have to compromise the types of foods you're preparing, their efficiency and freshness, and the intimacy of the evening you're aiming to create. You are hosting a dinner party, not a banquet.

a date and your star players, you've got a nucleus around which you can start inviting others. With the firm date, it's a *yes* or *no* question for the others. If they can't make it, it's their loss. Maybe next time. You move on down your list and still get the social credit for having extended an invitation. I advocate this over the guests-first model in which settling on a date means a dinner scheduled for two months in advance. People are busy. And that's okay.

But be careful — once guests know they are indispensible, they start throwing their weight around. They know they can request date and time changes. At the last minute they'll suggest putting the whole thing off for two weeks. I once attended a dinner party that started at five-thirty to accommodate new parents, who then left at seven. It was a thoughtful gesture to include the first-time parents, who probably need an eight to ten month grace period of gradual reintroduction to society. But without being explained in advance, it left the rest of us wondering why we were tired and eating cake before the sun had set.

But on some occasions the guest-first method is necessary, such as a gathering of work friends, or an anniversary that demands that certain people be there, or when you need to create a relaxed setting to ask friends if they'll donate genetic material for your test-tube baby. Just make sure that it's the occasion that is shaping the attendance, not a fear of excluding people. That way lies madness. Spending time with people we don't like is a hypocrisy we must endure in the workplace and among our families. But if we travel down that path in our own homes — at our own dinner tables — we are doomed.

The list of people we'd like to invite is most likely

comprised of friends and their partners. But let's spare a moment to take inventory, because there are archetypal characters that can make or break your dinner.

The Talker: This is the most important guest. Make a folder in your address book. Add to it anyone who is good at talking *and* listening — not necessarily an extroverted lout, but someone adept at talking to anyone. Once you have a collection of these types, make sure there is at least one at your dinner. The Talker is a spare tire, a lightning rod, who will engage other guests, allowing you to do those little things like cooking and serving.

The Bore: Don't confuse the Bore with the Talker. While the Talker has moderating skills and is able to get others to open up, the Bore only likes the sound of his own voice.

The Helper: Guests should never expect to work for their meal. But there are some people who just can't help helping. Take advantage. A good friend who will help clear plates or refill water without being told is invaluable.

The Turtle: It's not their fault, but some people just aren't good at talking. I would advise them to get good at listening. Often we cannot escape these people. They have married our friends and family and we need to embrace them. But they drain our energy and there should never be more than one at any table.

The Sommelier: Often derided as wine snobs, these are the people who will not only bring three bottles to dinner, but take responsibility for pouring and keeping everyone's glass full. An asset not to be abused, the sommelier can be counted on for major contributions without being asked.

The Drunk: We all have a friend who drinks too much. At the beginning of the night, they can be what we need to get things moving. But by the end of the night, guests will flee to escape their embarrassing behaviour. I have had great success in gently reminding a guest, "Kenny, please don't drink too much tonight."

The Sad Sack: Anyone who tells stories devoid of humour about something terrible that happened to them is not a good dinner guest. We all have family members suffering from tragic diseases. We all work for underfunded or understaffed organizations, but we've gotten together tonight to have a good time, not to commiserate.

The Wonderstruck: I know a few people who have their eyes wide open, entertained by every new idea that comes their way. Their enthusiasm and lack of cynicism not only makes them a joy to be around, but helps bring quieter people out of their shells.

The Snob: Forever putting a price tag on every moment, the Snob insists on comparing your meal with one he had in Bologna, your glasses with the ones at a hotel in Moscow. Invite the Snob only if you are a snob yourself and in competition with this person.

FRIENDS, FRENEMIES, AND PLUS ONES

 Single people do not automatically get a plus one. This is not to discriminate against the solo, but with only so much space at the table, a host may have just the right number of guests, precluding dates. Additionally, a host may reasonably not want to chance the chemistry of a cozy evening with someone they've never met.

Plus ones follow the same rules as wedding invitations, but with the host's advantage/excuse of having limited space. If a guest has a new boyfriend or girlfriend, he or she is confirming that it's a serious relationship by introducing them to the group (aka the jury). You can't bring a first date to the dinner party.

The dinner party is like a centrifuge for new friendships. It's going to take your personalities and spin them around at a speed powerful enough to separate the BS. This can be fantastic if you've got a friend, a co-worker, a co-worker's friend, a friend's wife, and you're thinking that maybe you might be actual friends, if only you got to know each other. It can be just the right setting to push past the barriers that we have around us at the office, but be warned. The dinner party can be like three friend dates in one. And the downside to that is that you can find yourself on the third date with someone you never would have talked to after the first. This can be a miserable circumstance. So if you're considering dinner with a couple and are experiencing strong waves of reasonable doubt about these people, go to a restaurant, where the difference between a two-and-a-half-hour meal and a four-hour meal will be money well spent.

Then there are the people that we already know we don't like. This is trickier and it's a question I get asked frequently. Can you invite a friend and tell her not to bring her husband? Sure, so long as you're comfortable with making it clear that you don't like her husband, you never want to see him, and you don't respect the choices she's made in her life. We don't have to invite into our homes anyone we don't like. Life is too short for that. However, most people are a package deal. We can't invite guests and tell them not to bring their husband or wife. That's a declaration of hostility.

If you truly can't stand your friend's husband, then you just can't invite her for dinner. That's it. The exception to this is a girls' night or boys' night or some other members-only-oriented celebration.

This is why it's so important that we like our friends' partners. Sure, we want our friends to be happy and in love. That's our reason on the books. But unofficially, we want them to date someone who isn't an idiot, a drunk, or a bore because we will have to endure this person for a lifetime of dinners, movies, and boat shows.

That's why there is so much weight put on the first time we meet a friend's new suitor. The moment your friend marries someone you don't like is the moment you stop being real friends.

Lest you think this is all too mercenary, remember that whom you invite to your dinner is more important than what you cook. It would be more fun to eat microwave popcorn with your best friend than a brilliant meal with Hitler.

THE INVITATIONS

The Time and Place

Technology comes and goes. Twenty years ago, we were forced to call each other to make plans. It put us on the spot. We'd pick up the receiver, attached by a coiled cable, and unbidden, we'd discover if our friends were slurring their speech at 9 p.m. Or we'd find out if we were indeed on an "it's me" level of friendship. Maybe in another twenty years, we'll all be cybernetically linked. Or maybe we'll have regressed to beepers or smoke signals.

But as of this moment in time, email is a perfectly good way to invite guests. The event is hardly urgent enough to merit a phone call. A text message — "cum 2 r house 4 dinner" — is too brief, and the form too demanding of an immediate reply. An e-vite is a clumsy relic of the last decade. And creating a Facebook event, as common as the practice may be, is overwrought for the occasion. You're trying to cook dinner for friends, not organize a union.

If you are emailing a group, do not hide any addresses. When I receive a dinner party invitation with all the other guests in the *bcc* line, I wonder if I'm being invited to the final scene in an Agatha Christie novel, where I'll be one of ten strangers, each with a plausible motive to have murdered Lord Snootington.

When sending out invitations, keep in mind what you would like to know as a guest. Maybe I'm paranoid, but the first piece of information I want to know is who else is coming. Believe it or not, not all of our friends like each other.

Include everyone in the address line. If you've already confirmed a couple of people, let others know that Couple A will be attending. For example, "Hey, we're hosting dinner on the 15th. Sue-Ellen and Pinter are coming (yes, they got a sitter for the night). We'd love it if you could join us. Does that night work for you?" This lets people know part of the guest list and, more importantly, that the date is set, so they can't respond by suggesting another date. If Marla's cousin's wedding rehearsal is on the 15th, then she can't come.

You don't need to list the time in the invitation. It's officious and can give people the impression that it's non-negotiable, like the date. The time has wiggle room (for the right people). If one person is working late that day, make it a later dinner rather than lose that guest.

Once people have confirmed, state a clear start time. None of this "sevenish" malarkey (see the punctuality chart in Chapter Five). I usually invite guests for 7 p.m. Keep in mind friends with children. They might need to start early or, if they have young children, they may need to start late so they can first put the kids to bed.

But do consider an addendum, reminding your friends not to drink and drive. Most people don't expect to get drunk at a dinner party, but it's pretty inevitable. Legal accountability differs depending on where we live, though our moral responsibility is the same: we should all act to prevent drunk driving when we can. We can't be wilfully ignorant of our guests, choosing to engage in criminal activity. If guests tell us that they will have to leak some military secrets or sell a bunch of cocaine in order to make it to dinner, we'd object to that. The invitation stage is a good point at which to address this rather than at the end of the night, when it will be an ugly argument over confiscating car keys.

Unintentionally, this divides us between urban and suburban. Where I live, if people are expecting to drink, they just take a cab. In the suburbs or rural areas, this is perhaps not an option. Some people may choose to drink more responsibly. Some may simply accept that intoxicated driving is a necessary part of owning a large house in the suburbs. But I have seen suburbanites call a car service to take a group of them to dinner, so I know it's possible.

Restrictions

Once guests have confirmed, ask them about their food restrictions. You'll need this information before you start planning your menu. No sense in researching pizza dough recipes only to find out that Elaine's husband has a severe gluten allergy. If your friends are vegetarians, make the meal vegetarian. If your friends are vegans, get new friends.

I use the word "restrictions," which can mean allergies, vegetarianism (in its infinite forms), religious dietary beliefs, dislikes, political boycotts, and other reasons, both legitimate and illegitimate. Wanting to be polite, most people won't list their dislikes, but they'll mention it once the offending dish is on the table. "It's funny that you made this porcini soup, because Jack just hates mushrooms," Jack's wife will say, rather than offering the information when it could have been helpful.

I had a guest tell me that he and his wife ate everything. Then the wife (because she was *cc*'d) reminded him that she was nine months pregnant and not eating raw foods, shellfish, or unpasteurized cheese. Be sure to ask both partners. Couples are notorious for speaking for each other and forgetting important details. This is why we *cc* people.

Guests will ask if there is anything they can bring. This is a big matzah ball, and I recommend tackling it now rather than at the last minute. If this is a potluck, then enjoy your anarchy.

The polite answer to this is, "You don't *need* to bring anything." Notice the emphasis on need. Of course, as the host, you wouldn't dream of putting any demands on your guests other than that they enjoy themselves. In reality, no adult goes to a dinner party empty-handed. Everyone over twenty-five knows this.

Guests, yes, you must bring something to a dinner party. The next time it seems too laborious to buy a bottle of wine, remember that in Japan, the cycle of gift-giving is so severe that if you return from a trip to Hokkaido without fake-milk-flavoured cookies for your co-workers, you will never get a promotion.

But you needn't spend too much. Remember that the gift can be helpful, but it can also be symbolic, a gesture of our gratitude for our host's efforts. A gift for the host can be anything — wine, flowers, fruit, a book, a card, a friendship bracelet, jam, unscented candles, a jar of Nutella (hint, hint), guajillo chilies, a copy of *Amazing Spider-Man* #50 to replace the one the host gave his niece as a birthday present when he was too broke to afford anything else, herbs from your garden, giant ice cube trays — but you can't show up empty-handed because you are an adult.

The easiest thing to tell guests is, "just wine." But if there are any gaps in your inventory, now is the time to fill them. If you want someone to bring dessert, just ask. Low on Riesling? Need cheese? Have a hankering for those almond cookies from your favourite bakery? Just ask, but do it now and be specific or you will get calls at 6:30 on Friday evening from the liquor store or bakery, asking you if you want German or Ontario Riesling, chocolate or cinnamon babka.

Guests, if your host is going all out with the meal, bring lots of wine. The average guest consumes two-thirds of a bottle over the course of dinner, so for a couple to bring one bottle between the two of them is cheap.

CEVICHE

The idea of ceviche — raw fish semi-cured in citrus juice — scares people off ever trying it at home, but let's do it in baby steps. It will illustrate not only that is there nothing to be afraid of, but that this is a simple, fun, easy dish to put together.

First, go to a fishmonger (or the person in charge of the fish counter at your supermarket) and tell them that you want a piece of something fresh enough to serve as tartare or ceviche. Raise an eyebrow as you tell them, "No skin and no pin bones," to suggest that you are serious, and that they will hear of it if you are not satisfied. Buy a couple of limes as well.

At home, slice the fish into bite-sized pieces. Squeeze some fresh lime juice over the top and sprinkle with a little salt. Watch as the colour and translucency change.

You have just made ceviche. We are going to get fancier and explore some more exotic variations. But before you get distracted by all that, or before you spend a day studying the process of denaturing (the juice of lemon or lime "cooks" the fish in a chemical process called denaturing, which breaks many of the bonds that hold protein molecules in their shape, changing the flesh from its plush, raw, translucent state to an opaque firmness), it's better to grasp and demystify the basic essentials of this dish.

That's all it is: citrus juice on seafood, which has an almost immediate effect. The thinner the fish, the quicker the citrus will permeate and change its flesh. If a piece of fish is the size of a grape, it should happen within a minute.

Once you've learned these basics — try this with at least one slice of fish to eliminate any nervousness about serving semi-raw seafood — move on to a traditional ceviche. This varies slightly across the Spanish-speaking countries where the dish is popular, but mostly it is whitefish with lime, chilies, onions, cilantro, and a few wedges of potato, sweet potato, or corn.

The ratio of ingredients will change from town to town and from day to day. Often, but not ideally, it is made in large batches and stored in the fridge. Finishing it with olive oil will slow the acid's effect on the fish, preventing it from getting mushy, but it's better to make it just before serving, letting the fish's freshness and flavour shine through.

I like to serve these two versions with warm, but not hot, rice (you don't want to put the cold fish over hot rice). Some form of starch, which could also just be the traditional potato wedges, is helpful to absorb the spice.

Tuna and Tomato Ceviche

2 tbsp.	gochujang (available in Asian grocery stores and many supermarkets)	30 mL
2 tbsp.	olive oil	30 mL
1/2 tsp.	sesame oil	2.5 mL
2 cups	cherry tomatoes, sliced in half	500 mL
1 lb.	tuna, cubed to the same size as the tomatoes (look for albacore or bigeye tuna)	450 g
2	limes, juice of	2
3	sprigs of oregano, leaves only	3
2	scallions, both white and green, finely sliced	2
	salt	

This is a variation I like to do in late summer, when tomatoes are in season.

In a mixing bowl, whisk the gochujang with the olive oil, sesame oil, and lime juice until it is the consistency of salad dressing (you can make this ahead of time). Add the remaining ingredients, reserving a pinch of the oregano and scallions. Mix and season with salt to taste. Sprinkle the remaining oregano and scallions over the top. Serve within a few minutes.

Makes four servings.

Tom Thai's Ceviche

1/2 cup	olive oil	125 mL
1	shallot, peeled and sliced into rings	1
1/2 lb.	sea bream, deboned and sliced into 1 in./2.5 cm-long strips	227 g
1/4	cucumber, diced	1/4
1/2	green mango, peeled and diced	1/2
1/4	Vidalia onion, diced	1/4
1/2	green Thai chili, deseeded and thinly sliced	1/2
1	red Thai chili, deseeded and thinly sliced	1
1	garlic clove, peeled and minced	1
1 tsp.	coarse salt	5 mL
1/2 tsp.	sugar	2.5 mL
1 tsp.	fish sauce	5 mL
2	limes, juice of	2
6	basil leaves, torn	6
6	mint leaves, roughly chopped	6
6	sawtooth leaves (long-leafed herb you might find in Asian grocery stores) or cilantro, roughly chopped	6

At his Toronto restaurant, Foxley, Tom Thai serves multiple variations on ceviche, often with Southeast Asian flavours. This particular one calls for sea bream, but you can substitute snapper, fluke, grouper, tuna, or halibut. Grouper and halibut are a bit denser, so if you're using a fish like that, let it sit in the citrus juice an extra minute or two.

Fill a small pot with olive oil, enough to cover the shallots. As counterintuitive as this may seem, slowly raise the heat with the shallots in the oil until near high. When the shallots have browned, remove them with a slotted spoon. Set them to dry on a paper towel. Sprinkle with salt.

Combine fish, cucumber, mango, onion, chilies, garlic, salt, sugar, and fish sauce in mixing bowl. Squeeze juice of limes over the top and mix. Let sit for one minute. Add herbs and crispy shallots. Mix and season to taste with salt. Serve with rice to cut the heat.

Makes four servings.

Bonus Tip: Look for limes with a smooth instead of bumpy skin. The bumpy ones tend to have more pulp and less juice.

CHAPTER TWO

THERE IS NOTHING INHERENTLY WRONG WITH A Moroccan meal. The country has a well-deserved reputation for layered spicing and slow-cooked succulence. But when Jesse invited me for a Moroccan dinner, he neglected to mention that he'd never been to Morocco, cooked Moroccan food, or even eaten Moroccan food. Pastilla is a challenging dish even if you know what you're doing. If it's made well, it doesn't seem odd that a pie of flaky pastry is filled with cinnamon-spiced squab (or chicken) and topped with icing sugar and almonds. The unusual addition of powdered sugar on chicken is probably something you should experience first if you're trying to approximate it at home.

"I hope this tastes good," Jesse said as he laid it on the table, "because I have no idea how it's supposed to taste." This did not inspire confidence in any of the guests, nor was it warranted. Despite his good intentions, we can all see what Jesse did wrong here.

THE MENU

Most people planning a dinner party make the same mistake of coming up with the concept before they are sure of their own capability. Often these ideas are the impetus of the dinner, inspiration gleaned from TV or magazines. But many hosts suffer from the opposite problem, which is not a lack of ideas, but an abundance of bad ones. Showtime finds them trying to reproduce the salsify wafer garnishes they saw in a cookbook by one of the world's greatest chefs.

If a friend invited me over, rubbed a chicken with salt and pepper, stuck it in the oven for forty-five minutes, and in that time boiled some potatoes and tossed a salad with olive oil and lemon juice, I would be a happy guest. But many of us want to be Nigella Lawson or Gordon Ramsay or that cartoon rat who has his own restaurant. Well, we're not all trained chefs, and that's okay because the projected image of the domestic diva or the bad-boy chef is about as authentic as that of the magical talking animal. As we gather ideas for our menu, let's start by being realistic.

Menus come to me in many ways. Sometimes I want to cook something because it has already proven popular, its ingredients are in season, it's easy to prepare or cost-efficient, I know my guests like it, it uses a new technique that I'd like to try, it's a combination of flavours I think might work, I already have it in my freezer, or it caught my eye in a book or magazine.

For some of us, menu planning is choosing to make the one thing we make well (which I thoroughly endorse). For some, it is poring over cookbooks. Others make spontaneous choices while walking through the market. There are many ways of choosing what goes on our menu. Some factors that determine our choices will be money, the theme, the style of meal, and incorporating food restrictions. Let's tackle these individually.

Money

Any time money is a factor, it should probably be discussed first, so let's talk about money. Rather than pretend that we can or should all become a television chef, some Botox-infused icon who cooks every luxury on a nebulous budget with the aid of invisible food stylists and celebrity guests, let's admit that money is a driving force in our lives and that we don't all have access to the same resources.

But the good news is that most of us, despite the paranoia that leads us to suspect otherwise, are surrounded by others in similar circumstances. If you are a twenty-two-year-old student, you probably live in a tiny apartment. Well, so do your friends. It is unlikely that any of your guests are Prussian nobility who will pop their monocle at the sight of a Triscuit. If you are a forty-four-year-old creative director at a marketing agency, guess what? You're middle-class, buddy. There's a reason why your friends are talking about vacations and their guilt over wanting private school for the kids. They are middle-class as well. If you are the CEO of a large corporation, then your life is probably populated by other wealthy people and by servants, like the person currently reading this for you.

So if we accept that we are surrounded mostly by peers of a similar economic bracket, it's time to stop projecting our need to climb beyond that. Having the boss over? Well, the boss knows that you make less money than her. That's how that power structure works.

Never spend money you can't afford to spend, and certainly don't do it for the sake of appearances. Anyone you need to ply with champagne isn't really your friend. Or it's a necessary business expense, in which case you can probably afford it.

The biggest monetary obstacle people complain about is buying wine. Pish posh. Expect guests to cover this. In the past year I've hosted fifty dinner parties. I've bought maybe a dozen bottles of wine. Guests bring wine. And the better your reputation as a host, the greater surplus you will accumulate. If you don't like the wine your guests bring, you're probably a wine aficionado, in which case you have a collection and can afford to share it.

One friend complained to me about the food cost of dinner parties. She said she'd spent $80 on fish for eight people. It turned out she was serving 8-ounce (227 g) portions of black cod, bought at $20 per pound. Personally, I don't want to eat a half-pound of anything. Are we at some 1950s steakhouse? She said the reasons for her portion sizes were fear of not having enough food and fear of looking cheap.

Also, she'd chosen to serve a large amount of the most expensive ingredient/course. Black cod is a pricey fish — why not skate or lake trout? And third, properly cooking a piece of fish demands too much of a host's time. It's not magic. It needs only a smoking hot pan and the patience to wait and flip the fish carefully once it's browned on one side. Anyone can do it once they are taught, but it requires too much attention at dinnertime. We can negate many of these obstacles by learning to cook foods that are both a good deal monetarily and a good deal less work to serve.

By this I mean we must learn to braise. Braising is slowly cooking something, submerged in liquid, at a low temperature, for a long time. Once the food is done, it is easy to reheat in a pan or in a pot of its original cooking liquid. What braising means to me is turning an inexpensive piece of meat (shoulder, leg, belly) into not just something delicious, but something that can be served with about five minutes' effort at mealtime. It is about freeing yourself from a steak that not only will cost four times as much, but will also require you to spend twenty minutes over the stove, poking, flipping, and checking, rather than hanging out with your guests. Mastering this technique can be the cornerstone of any successful dinner party. The menu stage is the time to make the choices that will ease, not complicate, the experience of hosting.

Themes

The theme of Jesse's meal was not really Moroccan, but rather the blind leading the blind. A themed meal is nice if there is a purpose behind it, not just a theme chosen at random. Please, unless there is an occasion, leave the themes to bachelorette parties and sixth seasons of sitcoms that have run out of ideas. Don't pick a theme just to do something different. This is like deciding to build a Lord of the Rings–themed bookshelf before learning to make a bookshelf. Doing things well should always take priority over fanciful ideas. Good food is always a good theme.

Style of Meal

There are many styles of service that we may or may not consider a dinner party: potluck, buffet, barbecue, picnic, hotpot, clambake, smorgasbord (okay, now we're just naming Elvis songs), but these are usually dining situations driven by external social forces, such as family celebrations or cottage weekends. A definition so broad might include going out to a restaurant. To call it a dinner party, invited guests need to be sitting together at a single table.

There are only two distinct styles of service that I would define as a dinner party: multi-course plated and family style. I like to switch between the two, often at the same dinner, serving one course as consciously composed plates for each guest, the next as a big bowl in the centre of the table from which they can all serve themselves. The Japanese say of their *nabemono* hotpot dish that the family who eats from the same pot grows closer. I see this happen all the time when dinner switches to family style. As people start reaching and passing, you can see their body language relaxing.

These are choices you can adjust through the planning and plating stages (see Chapter Seven). But now is the time to look at the bigger picture. If you want to serve courses, do you have enough plates to serve four dishes to six people? Are you prepared to wash dishes between courses if you don't have twenty-four plates? A dishwasher may be too slow and too loud. I wash cutlery between courses. It may seem fussy, but it's always appreciated. Sometimes I think we serve things family style to justify owning the large vessels at the top of our cabinets, the platter and bowl too gargantuan to fit on a proper shelf.

Food Restrictions

Despite what I said about vegetarians and vegans in the previous chapter, this is the perfect opportunity to show that you care. Make something special for people who have food restrictions. Consider balancing the needs of the few against the enjoyment of the many. If you've got one vegetarian or someone with a gluten allergy, plan a special dish for him or her, or even just a modification, but make sure to replace items rather than just serve them something with the good stuff missing. Making chili? It's not much more work to make a small veggie version on the side. Serving a braised short rib over a celeriac purée? Poach an egg for the vegetarian. If the majority are vegetarians, just make the whole meal meat-free.

If you know that someone has a severe nut or shellfish allergy, don't take any chances. Avoid any of those elements in the meal. Wash your preparation surfaces and tools thoroughly before starting to cook.

ON COOKBOOKS

When shopping for cookbooks, don't be swayed by flashy photography. Those photos are to your cooking what fashion spreads are to your gym routine. The stylized, micro-focus, glistening tomatoes, golden-crusted seared slices of foie gras, pea foam piped into an open pea pod, and symmetrically even zips of pistachio sauce create an unrealistic goal.

There's a reason why people call it food porn. Food photographers earn good money to give you a food boner for this stuff. But the idea that we, as amateurs, should attain the level of skill that professionals achieve is foolish and sure to lead to our disappointment.

Too many celebrity-driven cookbooks have not been properly recipe tested. If your town has a dedicated cookbook shop, ask the staff for suggestions. Don't trust cookbooks implicitly. Treat new cookbooks like a first date and don't take their word for anything, not the amount of salt or the baking time. But once you have cooked more than one dish out of a book and have been happy with it, trust the hell out of that book.

Here are suggestions for beginners from Mika Baraket, owner of the Good Egg cookbook store in Toronto, Ontario:

- *How to Cook Everything* by Mark Bittman. No photos, just a few instructional drawings. Chock full of info, facts, and figures as well as recipes. This is almost a textbook. Only men buy this book. Fact.

- *The Art of Simple Food* by Alice Waters. No photos or instructional illustrations, just a few spot drawings for flair. The recipes speak for themselves — very minimal on facts and figures, nothing fancy. Only women buy this one.

- *Cook with Jamie* by Jamie Oliver. Lots of photos. His dishes are not plated, but rather thrown on a plate simply and unpretentiously. We recommend this to students and young families.

- *The Cook's Illustrated Cookbook* by America's Test Kitchen. Instructional drawings, very didactic. This is for the older, studious cook.

- *Appetite* by Nigel Slater. Yes, there are photos, but more so of the ingredients than of the final dishes. This is the best cookbook ever written. If everyone read this, the world would be a better place.

THE PLAN

 Let me impress upon you the critical nature of this stage. If we take care to plan our shopping and cooking properly, we will ease our job as host, which should in turn relax our guests. Foolish are the hosts who bookmark a few recipes, thinking that they'll rise on Saturday, go out for brunch, take a leisurely stroll through the market, latte in hand, shop for ingredients, then spend the afternoon cooking.

The reason we plan ahead is to avoid a typical stressful dinner party scenario: Thirty minutes before guests arrive, the house is a mess, but you're on your way to the store because you don't have enough eggs to make the cornbread that needs forty minutes to bake.

Making Lists

I like to schedule my work with two lists, *Buy* and *Make*. My Buy list contains every item I need to make dinner, short of salt, pepper, and olive oil. It's obvious that we need buttermilk to make the cornbread because most of us don't keep buttermilk lying around. But do you think you have six cups of flour? Are you positive? Make sure before you start baking, so that you don't need to make an extra trip to the supermarket. On my Make list, I include every last kitchen detail, from soaking beans to making soup to slicing herbs. (You might make a third list, called *Clean*, if there are any major tasks here beyond a simple tidying.)

Let's break this down by looking at a sample menu for a recent dinner I hosted:

- Tunisian lamb thingee + couscous
- Kale salad + Yuzu dressing
- Beef cheek burgers
- Ask Jesse to bring dessert

For this dinner, my lists looked like this:

BUY

Lamb × 3 lbs.
Eggplant × 3
Onions
Garlic
Almonds
Dried apricots
Cilantro
Couscous

Kale
Arugula
Cheese (pecorino?)
Beef cheeks
Cheddar
Buns

<u>MAKE</u>

Thursday
  Lamb stew
  Beef cheeks: braise

Saturday
  Shave pecorino
  Chop kale
  Dressing

This is how I make my list. It's very sparse, but I try to write down everything, even if I know I have it. Then I'll go over it and cross things out before getting started. For example, I had couscous, almonds, apricots, and garlic. But if I didn't take the time to list them, I may have discovered later that I was mistaken, that I was out of almonds.

Never cook something because you think it will impress your guests. Instead, cook something you think tastes good. Never serve guests something that you haven't cooked before. Your friends will be too polite to tell you what you've done wrong when you serve them overcooked, over-salted food, but you will know. If you are thinking of serving a dish at a dinner two weeks from now, test it out tonight. The heads of two can be felled with but one stroke of the sword, or is "two birds with one stone" the more related expression? You get a weeknight meal out of it and you'll learn how to properly execute a dish. In the kitchen, we learn more from our mistakes than from our successes.

Personally, I break this rule regularly, but I host a dinner every week. My usual formula is: one dish that I know is a crowd-pleaser; one dish that may be a tweak, but still reliable; and something new and experimental. It's only because I do this all the time that I feel comfortable failing in front of an audience. When I'm hosting friends, I don't take chances — nothing from the new album. No improv. Only hits.

High-end restaurants serve an *amuse-bouche,* a one- or two-bite dish. Using either bold flavour or the simplicity of fresh ingredients, the *amuse* says to the diner, "You are in for a good meal. Trust your host." Take that into consideration if you're organizing a multi-course meal. Not the pretension of an *amuse,* and certainly not the uptight theatricality of calling it that, but the idea behind it. Make sure the first thing that hits the table leaves a strong impression. If it's a lentil soup, it should be a killer lentil soup, balanced with lots of acidity and spice.

To an Italian cook, the order is predetermined: soup, antipasti, pasta, fish, meat, cheese, and dessert. But serve people food in the order that will make them happiest. If you want to start with pancakes, so be it. This country was founded on that principle.

That "lamb thingee" on this menu was a Moroccan lamb stew I got from Hugh Fearnley-Whittingstall's cookbook *The River Cottage Meat Book.* It definitely tastes better the day after it's cooked, once all the flavours have mingled. So not only did I prep it before Saturday (my list says Thursday just because that's an evening I had free), but I did a double batch, froze half, and saved it for another dinner. Same goes for the beef cheeks. I braised a whole batch on Thursday, about four pounds, set aside what I needed for Saturday, and froze the rest.

For this menu, I've chosen dishes that are all prep-heavy. On Thursday, I spend several hours cooking, sure. That's my Thursday night. But on the day of the dinner, I just need to chop some greens and make a dressing. Each course will require me to be in the kitchen for only a maximum of fifteen minutes, and I don't need more than an hour, tops, to prep.

All of this may sound counterintuitive. If we are hosting dinner on Saturday, why aren't we spending Saturday in the kitchen? But set aside a weekday evening to accomplish most of the work for a prep-heavy menu and it will not just alleviate your time pressures on the day of the party, but eliminate any doubts about how much time you'll need. Having a schedule for each task will reduce your worrying. You can wake up Saturday and relax with the paper, eat brunch, and watch cartoons, knowing that you don't need the whole day in the kitchen to get ready for dinner.

Planning and advance work will also free up space so that you're not using every pot, bowl, and inch of counter at once. If a soup can be made ahead of time, get it done so that space is freed up in the kitchen on the day that you need it.

When I'm cooking from a recipe I haven't made before, I start by reading it out loud and (yes, I know this sounds silly) miming the motions. It's goofy, sure. We all have different styles of learning. For me, it helps to rehearse it. When I pretend to scoop down the sides of my mixer, I get a better sense of what's involved in the recipe. It helps pinpoint the elements that I'm less certain of, while familiarizing me with the recipe.

Quantities

When we're fixing ourselves a snack, we know just how much we want. But when we're planning dinner for six, it's difficult to know how much to make. We're afraid of making too little.

You can estimate by weight, volume, or fistful. You can imagine how much you would like to eat of every item. You can plan it out based on governmentally approved nutrition charts, calculating how many grams or ounces of meat, vegetable, grains, dairy, or candy each person needs. You might try visualizing a single plate, piled high with everything you're serving. That might snap you out of the phobia that there won't be enough food.

When I'm planning proper meals, I strategically place the heaviest dishes toward the end. I also try to make it something with a negotiable amount. Guests may be more full than you'd expected, and no one wants to see good food go to waste, certainly not expensive pieces of fish. It can be hard to estimate how much people will eat (see Chapter Two: The Plan and Chapter Eight: The Portioning). This is something you will learn with experience. To begin, it's better to have too much than not enough.

For budgetary reasons, we can't simply have too much of everything. So whatever you're going to have an excess of, make it something you wouldn't mind eating as leftovers, not something you'll resent having spent too much on.

One time I hosted a meal in a movie theatre. How much caramel corn does a dozen people eat during a matinee? How much bucatini with tomato sauce? Who knows? I chose these things because I could prepare them in advance, and because they were so inexpensive that I could afford to make far too much. For dinner, I might make my last course a lamb ragù with polenta. If we are full, I can serve only half of the ragù and freeze the rest. The polenta is dirt-cheap. Consider this while planning your meal, rather than leaving expensive pieces of fresh meat or fish for a final course that guests may be too full to eat, though even a big piece of rib-eye can be trimmed down at the last minute. Individual quiches cannot.

Or you can accept that, as samurai philosopher Musashi Miyamoto liked to say, "you must practise this." Just start by making too much. Eventually, you'll develop a sixth sense for how much guests need.

Just remember that people will eat more of food served family style than the same dish served as a plated course. A dish with three asparagus spears, three maple syrup–roasted sunchokes, and three slices of rare rib-eye is a perfectly good plate of food. But if you put out a platter of that, multiplied by the number of guests, those amounts seem skimpy. With shared plates, people always start off by taking too large a portion. Perhaps that's a vestige of the family element of family style. When we were kids, in competition with our brothers and sisters, we helped ourselves to big portions and ate fast, so that we could have more of the good stuff.

Presentation

How will you serve the food you've chosen? What will it look like on the plate? When you're at a restaurant and you see a chef spooning out sauce, mounting a deep-fried puck of something, coaxing a piece of fish out of a pan, then topping it all with a slaw he freshly tossed with dressing, you know that he didn't just decide how to plate it at the last minute. That's a dish he has served many times every night, and he has done so for many weeks or even months.

Once you know what you're going to serve, decide how you'll serve it. Sketch it out on paper. No, you don't need a blueprint or 3D animatics to storyboard how a steak will look with a potato next to it. But if you're composing a real dish, take a few minutes to conceive how it will look. It's better than figuring it out while hungry guests wait at the table.

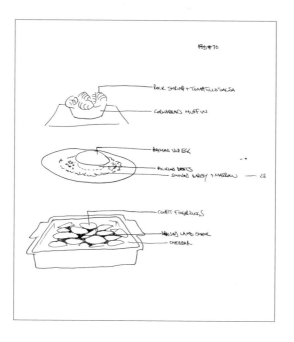

Also, if your dishes have multiple elements on them, it's helpful to have an illustrated guide as a checklist. It can help you avoid forgetting to include key ingredients. I've made that mistake, serving a tuna ceviche with horse-radish, only to find I had forgotten the horseradish. Attach your drawing to the fridge with magnets.

ON WINE

I once hosted a dinner (at which I was not cooking) for a group of chefs. About half of them were very into wine and the other half were not, several saying that they'd just as soon have beer with this meal. The chefs who weren't interested in or didn't know about wine were proud of this, professing a belief common among young chefs that they need not understand anything outside of a kitchen.

During the main course, a slow-roasted saddle of lamb, one of the chefs, a Frenchman, poured us a wine he'd brought. We all agreed that the wine was good and that the lamb tasted even better with the pairing. Then he poured us a drink from another bottle of the same wine, one that he'd opened an hour earlier. The effect dumbfounded many of the chefs at the table, all of whom agreed that what had been a very good dish was now a great dish.

There are two lessons in this story:

1. Chefs, even good ones, can be ignorant about wine, and that's nothing to be embarrassed about.

2. The most basic understanding of wine pairing can dramatically elevate a meal.

If you are a wine person, wine snob, wine collector, sommelier, wine steward, wine captain, or wine lieutenant, skip this sidebar. You already have separate glasses for Pinot Noir. You have a wine collection that you store at 54°F (12°C), possibly in your basement cellar, a temperature-controlled cabinet in the kitchen, or a storage locker you rent because you're very wealthy. You know which wines to serve with which foods and how to pour them.

For the rest of us, let's simplify things.

When choosing a wine to drink with dinner, most of us have no idea what we're doing. We take refuge in that old refrain, "I may not know art, but I know what I like." Pleased with a particular wine we've enjoyed, we remain loyal.

When eating in restaurants, I defer to the good sense of sommeliers. That's their job. When eating at home, I defer to the tastes of my friends, who bring most of the wine. But I keep a few things on hand, versatile wines that pair well with groups of flavours. We don't need to become masters at pairing wine and food, but some basic education can go a long way.

The common mistake people make with wine pairing, promoted by the axiom of white wine with fish, red with meat, is thinking that these basic food elements are natural partners with some wines. The marketers who write the pairing suggestions on wine labels capitalize on that. According to those labels, just about every wine goes great with chicken or fish.

But it's the flavours and characteristics of the dish — sweet, sour, spicy, bitter, salty, umami — with which we are balancing the wine. Why would we expect the same wine to go as well with chicken Kiev as with jerk chicken? Also, other than a 1960s hotel chef or a first-year culinary student, who is serving chicken Kiev?

I've always got a couple bottles of Riesling chilled in the fridge. These off-dry wines will balance well with acidic or spicy foods. Whereas a fiery curry would just demolish the subtleties of a Cabernet Sauvignon, the red wine would go well with the richness of a rare piece of red meat.

A good wine shop has someone on hand who knows the product. If it's really important to find a wine that pairs well with a particular dish, ask for help. Read newspaper columns by local wine writers, who know what's in stock where you live. Contact them for advice. People who love wine want other people to love wine and are often eager to share their knowledge.

And we don't have to drink wine. There are lots of foods that just go better with beer — the briny vitality of oysters or mussels; the heat of pozole; the gummy smoke of a deli sandwich — not to mention that some foods, such as barbecue, just don't fit with wine, practically or aesthetically. No one feels right gripping a sticky pork rib in one hand and tearing at the flesh while daintily holding a wineglass by the stem in the other.

I would caution against adding a pre-dinner cocktail to the evening. A well-made cocktail demands great care and precision. It's not the best thing to be doing when you should be paying that attention and care to your guests. If you really like the idea of having a cocktail before dinner, and it's a very classy prelude that I endorse, stick with punch. You can make it in advance and serve it from a bowl as guests arrive. See the end of Chapter Five for a great recipe.

PTITIM AND CHEESE

In support of my theory that we would rather have simple
food with good friends than fancy food with enemies, I present mac and cheese. A well-made macaroni and cheese, by
which I mean lots of cheese, should appeal to the comfort
food pleasure centres of most North American brains. To jazz
it up, and to suggest to your guests that you've gone to some
extra effort (without actually making any extra effort), replace
the macaroni with another type of pasta.

Ptitim, commonly known as Israeli couscous, is not actually
couscous, which is made from semolina. Ptitim is wheat pasta
in the shape of small balls. Its scoopability makes it ideal for
being baked with a cheese sauce.

The appeal of this type of dish is that once it's assembled,
it only needs to be slid into the oven during dinner. I like to
serve it with similarly low-maintenance foods, such as sausages or rapini.

Ptitim and Cheese

2 cups	ptitim (aka Israeli couscous aka Icelandic orzo)	500 mL
3 tbsp.	butter	45 mL
2 cups	milk	500 mL
2 oz.	flour	57 g
1/3 lb.	Cheddar cheese, grated	150 g
1/3 lb.	Manchego cheese, grated	150 g
	salt	
	white pepper	

In a large pot of salted, boiling water, cook the ptitim until
soft, but not mushy, about fifteen minutes. Strain. Mix with 1
tbsp. (15 mL) butter. Spread on a baking sheet to cool.

In a sauce pot, gently warm the milk without boiling it.

Melt the remaining butter in a large pot on low heat. To make a roux, add flour and mix with a spatula. The flour and butter will solidify into a ball. Stir it around the pot for a few minutes to let the flour toast a bit. The roux will thicken your sauce. Just remember that it's equal parts of fat and flour, so if your sauce is too thin, just make another roux with equal amounts of butter and flour.

Add the milk and whisk until there are no clumps. Add the cheese and stir. Add the ptitim, mix thoroughly, season with salt and white pepper to taste, and pour into a baking dish (if you have individual ramekins so that each guest can have his or her own, go for it).

Allow the mixture to cool at room temperature. Cover and refrigerate. The day of the dinner, remove from the fridge. During the meal, heat the oven to 350°F (175°C). Bake, covered, for thirty minutes. Remove the cover and continue baking until the top browns, about thirty minutes, or about twenty minutes if cooking in ramekins.

Serves four.

CHAPTER THREE

BEING A PREPARED HOST IS NOT BEING AN OBSES-
sive. It's done out of consideration for our guests.
Have you ever been to a party where the host is not
ready for you? Of course you have. I had this experience
just a couple of days ago. And it'll happen again and again.

I showed up at the invited time. The hosts said hello,
then disappeared into the kitchen, where they spent half
an hour assembling bruschetta. We're talking about tomatoes and basil on toast, a five-minute operation.

I've shown up on time to find the hosts peeling potatoes.
What were they doing earlier in the day? Having brunch?
Taking Junior to soccer practice? Sleeping in? Whatever it
was, it was more important than looking after their guests.

As we delve into the domestic chores of shopping, cooking, and cleaning — the real work of a dinner party — remember that all this effort is for someone else's enjoyment. I would rather have a host who hangs out with me and overcooks a steak than one who spends all night in the kitchen creating the perfect meal. I mean, I'd rather have both. But this is an either/or world.

THE SHOPPING

Make Two Trips

This is why we scheduled a Saturday dinner. For most working people, cooking, cleaning, and getting ready for company within two hours of leaving the office on a Friday is impossible — it's simply not enough time.

Even if you've got a full day to prepare, it may be advantageous to make two separate shopping trips to allow yourself even more time in advance. I understand this seems crazy to a lot of people. It would have been crazy to me when I was a kid. I grew up in a household where my father and I went grocery shopping every Thursday night. But it now seems strange to me that a household could purchase fresh produce only once every seven days unless they are subsisting on cabbage.

To make the most of your time will probably mean two shopping trips. As we saw in the menu and planning stages, we can reduce our stress and workload on the day of the dinner by choosing prep-intensive dishes and preparing them ahead of time — any time you're braising, brining, stewing, or pickling, do it first. Those items usually make up 90 percent of my shopping. Some items, such as fish and green vegetables, need to be as fresh as possible. But when you're organized and you've already done most of your work, a quick run to buy red snapper and basil is not a huge inconvenience, particularly if, on the day of your dinner, that's pretty much all you have to do.

Know Your Butcher

It's become a cliché, but knowing your merchants will pay unexpected dividends. Befriend your grocer, butcher, and fishmonger, and you will receive fresher cuts and rare items.

Unless you are shopping for meats in the Slim Jim aisle at a 7-Eleven, your supplier has specialists. Even in a major supermarket, there are humans with these titles. Every big store has people in charge of its sections.

When you are on a first-name basis, they will tell you the days that specific products arrive so you can get them at their freshest. They will offer you specialty items that they have only in small quantities. If it is a small shop, they will special order items for you, not for profit, but as a favour.

Yes, this is easy for me to say. I live near an area of Toronto known as Kensington Market for a reason. A remnant of the early twentieth century, when Jewish merchants lived downtown, the neighbourhood is still home to dozens of independently owned shops that sell produce, meat, fish, cheese, coffee, and bread, as well as tattoos, vintage clothing, and nutritional supplements.

Obviously I'm not advocating for everyone in North America to move to my 'hood. But wherever you live, there is more than one choice for buying food.

Your city might have a still active market district, such as Jean Talon in Montreal, Chelsea Market in Manhattan, Quincy Market in Boston, or Granville Market in Vancouver. More than likely it has big-chain supermarkets, small neighbourhood grocers, specialty shops, an expensive supermarket in the rich neighbourhood, and perhaps a Chinatown. What I'm saying is, start shopping around — be promiscuous with your food money.

Shopping is an opportunity to practise flexibility. If your menu comes from a cookbook, it may contain out-of-season items that aren't available, or obscure items that are hard to find. This is something that stymies a lot of novice cooks. I remember cooking for one of the first times and calling my girlfriend's dad to ask what a shallot was. When I'm reading a magazine like *Art Culinaire*, I understand that the recipes are for chefs only, and that I'm not expected to track down sodium hexametaphosphate.

Recipes are guidelines, not the word of God. We are free to reinterpret them. A red onion is a suitable substitute for a shallot, but not a good substitute for lobster. Spinach is a fine replacement for escarole. But it's difficult to make those choices without a comfortable understanding of food.

The people at your local supermarket should be able to advise you in this area. No, they shouldn't be expected to carry every cultivar of mango. But if they don't know that button, crimini, and portobello mushrooms are all the same mushroom at different stages of growth, they

STRESS BRAISING

 So many of us bake to relax, but what do we do with all the cookies and cupcakes? When we fill our spare moments with baking, it becomes counter-productive to the time we spend at the gym. Bringing sweets to the office makes us popular. But at some point we are fattening people up and then we have to listen to our co-workers babble on about their failed diets. The other problem with stress baking is that it doesn't freeze well.

Consider stress braising. When I'm upset, I don't want to eat or write or be around people, but I don't mind cooking. Braising, as we've established, is a method best done in advance and it stores well in the freezer.

The next time you're frustrated with your idiot children, thoughtless boss, or boorish neighbour, and you're thinking of whipping up something with butter, flour, and eggs, head to the butcher shop. Pick up some pork belly, lamb shoulder, or beef cheeks. Throw them in a pot with onions, celery, and carrots, cover with water or wine, chuck it in the oven and get back to your life. The actual labour is so minimal. I don't know about you, but I like shopping. Heading into the market to pick up one or two items is quality time alone.

When you pull a quivering mound of meat from its braising bath, slice off a little taste with a butter knife, sprinkle some salt, and let the fat melt on your tongue, you'll be astonished at how little effort it was. Cooled and wrapped, these pucks of meat will stack up in your freezer. Removing them will feel like paying for a vacation with money that you've responsibly saved.

The problem with braising is that no one wants to make preparations for tomorrow. Few people take the advice to braise today to eat tomorrow. They just hear the cooking time of four to six hours, then try to cut that short at the last minute. They end up popping a leg of lamb in the oven without enough time before dinner, braising it for three and a half hours, and then wonder why it's not tender enough.

I get it. We're all busy just trying to put food on the table today. Hosting a dinner party means devoting our spare time to make a special evening. If it were easy and effortless, it would be called watching TV.

are poorly trained or lousy employees. If they can't tell you which apples are sweet and which are tart, stop shopping there.

And always ask merchants about carrying new products. Multiple requests will result in them making additions to their inventories.

THE PREP

 Last minute is the worst minute. Anything you can do in advance, do it. Thirty minutes before your guests arrive, you should be sitting, relaxing with a drink (see Chapter Four). Don't answer the door by saying, "Oh, no, I was hoping you'd be late because I'm not ready."

Before you begin to prep, clear your workspace as much as possible. Too often our workspace in our homes is defined as that one square foot of surface that is clean, the accidental eye in the hurricane of junk. To work efficiently, this area must be free of not just newspapers, schoolbooks, DVD covers, and vintage Spider-Man roller skates, but jars of fancy salt, rarely used kitchen appliances, nearly consumed wine bottles, bags of rice, clementines, or whatever other items you may have on your kitchen counter. These things should be on shelves. The workspace is for working.

Wear an apron, preferably one that covers your upper body. Or better yet, wear B-list clothes to cook in, as you would for painting. I find that wearing a cooking outfit helps differentiate the time spent prepping. It marks a clear division between this type of work and being presentable for company, not that anyone needs to dress up for company. (But you know you can't be sweaty, right?)

Place a wet cloth under your cutting board to keep it from slipping. Wash your board and knife after each task to prevent cross-contamination and flavours from transferring to each other. No one wants a guest to ask how you got the peaches to taste like onions.

Gem paks (aka deli cups or jam paks) are those universal-sized (8 oz./250 mL, 16 oz./500 mL, 32 oz./1 L) clear plastic containers that restaurants use to store their prep. You get them from supermarkets and delis when you buy stuff like cream cheese or capers, or you can buy them at a restaurant supply store, where they'll be inexpensive, or online where they are widely available in bulk. They will save you so much space and aggravation. Using masking tape and marker, label every container with the date.

Most of us have a cupboard filled with a collection of mismatched Tupperware: round, square, tall, short; the oblong one for asparagus; the thimble-sized one we use for a teaspoon of leftover sauce we want to put in the back of the fridge and forget forever; the one with the red, oily stain that we use only when all the other containers are in use; the one without a lid; the one with the cartoon duck that we like to use for our lunches and we get mad if someone else uses it to entomb a baked half-potato.

What's great about deli cups is that they're uniform in shape, cheap, and disposable. Once we convert to these for storage, we don't have to play fridge Jenga, trying to stack our Dirty Dozen ragtag group of misfit plastic containers so that there is room for a six-pack of beer. Because they are

TEN TIPS

Now that you're ready to cook, here are ten tips that will improve your game.

1. READ RECIPES THOR-OUGHLY BEFORE COOKING.

You don't have to memorize them, but if you know them well enough that you could tell a friend, it'll save you time when cooking. It's maddening to keep running back to the book while you've got something on the stove.

2. WHETHER THIS IS ADVANCE PREP OR DAY-OF PREP, GO THROUGH YOUR LIST AND ORGANIZE IT BY CHRONOL-OGY.

Let's say your list says: cook barley, cook kidney beans, portion tuna, chop cilantro and basil, juice lemons, chop onions and garlic, roast beets and peel. Some of this stuff takes a long time. Some of it is quick. Some of it can sit for a long while once prepared, and some of it needs to be as fresh as possible. Because the beets, beans, and barley will need to cook for at least a half, hour, deal with them first. This

is even more important if you're boiling a number of items, as we are here. Most of us have only one large pot, which is all the more reason to get the process started as early as possible.

3. LEARN TO COOK DRIED BEANS.

Beans are delicious, good for you, and so cheap they're practically free. Soak them overnight. Boil them at a low simmer.

4. WHEN GRAINS, BEANS, POTA-TOES, OR ANY BOILED ITEM IS COOKED, STRAIN AND COOL IT THE RIGHT WAY BY SPREADING IT OUT ON A FLAT SHEET.

And don't refrigerate until cool. Hot things poured into a bowl continue to cook. Hot things placed into the fridge steam the foods around them.

5. BE EASY ON YOUR HERBS.

Cilantro is hearty as hell. Whack it up at 9 a.m. and it'll be just as vibrantly green at dinnertime. But basil will take any excuse to bruise and wilt. If you have a super-sharp knife and a soft touch, you can finely slice it earlier and cover it with a damp cloth; otherwise, save this one for the last minute. Mint, parsley, and dill are durable as well. Rosemary browns. It's usually cooked, but if you're garnishing with it, chop at the last minute if you want it to remain green. Same with tarragon, which darkens, rather than browns. Oregano leaves are small and should only be separated, not chopped.

6. CITRUS JUICES TASTE THEIR BEST WHEN THEY ARE FRESHLY SQUEEZED. If you're making ceviche, squeeze that lime straight onto the fish.

7. DON'T OVERCROWD YOUR PAN. The concept of over-crowding the table translates to cooking as well. If the recipe says to brown meat in batches, it means that the surface area of metal must be on a high heat to achieve the proper colour and flavour. That browning is called a Maillard reaction. Put too much in the pan at once and the temperature drops. The meat turns grey instead of brown.

8. DON'T FUSS. Once at work I was tossing something in a pan because I'd just learned to confidently flip and I wanted to show off. My chef reminded me that every time I shake or move the pan, I'm taking it off the heat. Keep your pan on the heat. Move it only when you have to. And in the name of Zeus, leave a searing piece of meat alone. If you've placed a piece of animal flesh in a hot pan with some fat, it will stick to the surface. When seared, it will release. Bother it before that, and the flesh will tear.

9. THINK TWICE ABOUT SLIC-ING A ROAST AT THE TABLE. The juices will run everywhere and of course you never know if it's cooked the way you want until it's been sliced into. When a roast is done, bring it to the table so everyone can see. It needs to rest before being carved. When it's ready, you'll find it easier to bring it back to the kitchen, slice it up, and assemble on the platter.

10. TASTE EVERYTHING, AT EVERY OPPORTUNITY. Short of raw chicken, you should poke your finger and dig a spoon into everything as you go. Unless you have the sixth or seventh senses of telepathy or precog-nition, use the five senses you have. When you taste a sauce or salad as each ingredient is added, you will know when and where you went right or wrong.

all the same and can be bought for about twenty-five cents apiece, we don't mind giving them away with leftovers.

In my home they're on my shelf, storing dry ingredients (cumin, guajillo chili, black pepper, pumpkin seeds, raisins). They're in my fridge, storing leftovers (salsa, guacamole), with strips of masking tape that clearly label or date duck fat, pickled onions, or canned chipotles (you were *not* going to throw the tin in the fridge with cling wrap over the top). My freezer is stacked top to bottom with them, making it easy to shift things around when I need a serving of parsnip purée or mole, chicken stock or tomato sauce.

As they come in sizes roughly equal to 1, 2, or 4 cups (250 mL, 500 mL, or 1 L), they're good for estimating amounts as well. When I'm prepping for dinner, rather than a mess of bowls, each filled with a little garlic, onion, or parsley, the 1 cup (250 mL) containers allow me to keep all my prep separate, all the ingredients for one dish piled in a neat column.

I could tell you to do as many things simultaneously as possible or I could caution you against doing too much at once. Both are true. A good cook is efficient, doing as much at once as possible, wasting no time. Waiting for something to boil? Peel the next thing on the list. Waiting for something to cool? Wash the dirty pots.

But a good cook also doesn't attempt to do so much at once that food is forgotten and burns or, worse, they have an accident with knives. Know your limits and work within them. Many of us are forgetful of what's not in front of us. If you need to, set a timer for foods in the oven.

As I write this, I've got my oven at 250°F (120°C). Beets are roasting and pork belly is braising. I know I'm not going to forget them because it's making my apartment uncomfortably hot. But every time I brine chicken overnight, I leave a note on my bathroom mirror that says, "Rinse that chicken off, dummy."

At the very latest, you should plan your prep to be completed thirty minutes before showtime. That leaves time for emergencies — for making something again because you burned it or there wasn't enough.

THE CLEANING AND THE SETTING

 Your house does not need to be professionally cleaned just because you're having guests over. Everyone owns sneakers, children's toys, and umbrellas. Your friends do, too. We understand this. And unless you live in an ultra-modern showroom for Danish furniture, a science lab, or a recreated set from Stanley Kubrick's *2001*, some of that humanity is going to show. Don't worry about concealing every last trace of your possessions. But that doesn't mean you have to be a slob. A dirty toilet or sink is embarrassing.

Any room that guests will be in should be neat. Not spotless, but neat. That means the living room, dining room, and kitchen, and especially the bathroom. That is the room that guests will be in alone, with the time to notice that your mirror is covered in whatever ejects from your teeth as you floss. Make sure that the sink, toilet, and mirror are scrubbed.

I had an uncle who kept his porn stash in the guest bathroom, probably so his wife wouldn't find it. Instead, I found it, every year on Passover. In case there are any technophobes out there who still own non-digital pornography, do not store it in the guest bathroom, where a guest might uncover it while searching for spare toilet paper.

And do have spare toilet paper. Leave not even the slightest chance of subjecting a guest to the humiliation of that shortage.

Depending on what type of table and chairs you have, give them a once-over to make sure guests aren't sitting in gum or other residues. No one cares if your bedroom is messy, even if you are using it to store coats. Rather than preoccupy yourself with steam cleaning the sofa and dusting every shelf, just try to keep surfaces free of clutter.

Many people have books or magazines on their coffee table. But if you expect guests to put drinks on it, your collection of *New Yorker*s and vintage *Life* magazines are in the way. We get it — you read this week's review of the biography of Lincoln. But if guests sit on a sofa, they will want a place to put their drinks down. The coffee table or side tables must be free of your belongings.

Your kitchen should be spotless, not just for appearances or hygiene, but for your ease of use. Some space, not needed for cooking, should be cleared and dedicated for the wine or flowers that your guests will bring. Left to their own devices, they will put these things exactly in the middle of your workspace. You could be doing your last-minute chiffonade of basil and guests will drop a bouquet of lilies right on the cutting board.

If you are one of those people who insist on having every conceivable accoutrement of Victorian refinement, then knock yourself out. Lay down three forks, two spoons, and two knives. Wedge napkins into silver napkin holders. Assemble a diorama in the table's centre that depicts the history of table setting.

But I'm a minimalist. I believe the only things that belong on the table are the tools we need for eating dinner. For me, that usually means wineglasses, water glasses, napkins, cutlery, and candles. But it can depend on the evening and the meal. If you've made pizza — and congratulations on making dough from scratch — you don't need any cutlery. If you've made some Asian noodle dish, put out chopsticks. The word "utensil" stems from *utensilia*, Latin for "things for use." They are tools, not decoration. Don't put out tools you don't need.

To start, the table will be set for the first course and nothing more. The seven-piece cutlery setting is a waste of space. If the first course requires a knife and fork, that's how it's set up. If it's a shared dish and guests will help themselves, there are side plates and serving spoons or tongs.

When I was a kid, setting the table meant first laying out the padded table cover, then the tablecloth to cover that. It made me question the value of my father's oak table, since we never saw it during dinner. So I also don't believe in tablecloths.

When I was ready to purchase my first grown-up table, I chose a block of reclaimed factory wood, its surface gouged with fifty years of labour but preserved under a coating of enamel. There is no need to protect it with table-cloths, placemats, or coasters — not that it has stopped anyone from giving me those items as gifts.

If your table is a type of wood, such as teak, that will stain from the weight of a napkin or if you talk too loud near it, then these measures are all necessary. Have your protective equipment out, counted, and checked for stains. If you've got a sturdy, stain-resistant table, consider doing away with this junk. Like a condom, it spoils the mood. And there is literally zero chance of your cutlery getting pregnant from an unprotected table.

Candles, however, are a must. Maybe they seem like the affectation of a 1990s goth kid or a romance novel. And the older we get, the more we are likely to have spent money on effective track lighting and lamps for our home. But the dramatic effect of candlelight is the best atmosphere you could ever buy, and it only costs a couple of dollars.

Avoid tea lights, those thimble-sized pucks of wax. They are too small and usually burn for only ninety minutes. If the evening goes on for four hours, you'll have to keep lighting new ones. It's not worth it. Go to a restaurant supply store (the same one where you got your deli cups from) or a supermarket and get some six-hour candles. Light them fifteen minutes before showtime and place them in glass jars (save jars from jam or honey) or bowls so they're not easily blown out (by haughty people like myself, who derisively snort with gusto sufficient to extinguish candles).

One of the biggest factors that determines our perception of restaurants is lighting. Harsh overhead light makes us feel like we're in a dentist's office. Soft light, twinkling and reflecting from multiple points, makes us feel attractive. So while you're at it, install a dimmer on your dining room's overhead light switch. This will cost no more than a few dollars, is available at any hardware store, and can be installed even by someone like me (though I did have a grown-up do mine).

BRAISING: TWO RECIPES

I've talked a lot about braising, but let's get practical. Here are a simple guide to braising and two recipes that make use of the meltingly soft meat. Both of these dishes are on my regular rotation of crowd-pleasers.

Here we are working with beef cheek. You'll find the same techniques work with other meats (after you learned to tie your shoes, you didn't need to relearn with every new pair), but for light-coloured pork, chicken, or rabbit, use white wine instead of red, and don't caramelize the vegetables.

Braised Beef Cheeks

1 tbsp.	fat (vegetable oil, grapeseed oil, or duck fat)	15 mL
3 lbs.	beef cheeks (about 4 cheeks)	1.36 kg
1	onion, peeled and quartered	1
1	carrot, peeled and quartered	1
2	garlic cloves, peeled	2
1 cup	red wine	250 mL
4	sprigs of thyme	4
1	bay leaf	1
1 tsp.	black peppercorns	5 mL
	water to cover	

You will need a large lidded container that can go in the oven. A stainless steel pot or a casserole will do, but you can also cook this in a countertop Crock-Pot.

The first two steps are optional. Browning the meat and caramelizing the vegetables will give you more flavour and colour, but you could just dump it all in a pot and cover it with water.

Preheat the oven to 275°F (135°C).

Heat a frying pan on high until it's smoking. Melt just enough fat to lubricate the pan. In batches, sear beef on each side until a crust develops, about one minute a side. Transfer to the pot. When searing, add more fat as the pan dries.

Reduce the pan to low heat. Add the onion, carrot, and garlic. Stirring occasionally, caramelize in the pan. It'll take about forty-five minutes. Transfer the vegetables to the pot. Deglaze the pan with wine, then pour into the pot. Add the remaining ingredients and just enough water to cover the meat. Beef floating at the surface will dry, so use an oven-safe dish to weigh it down (in my kitchen I've got a small pot lid that's just the right size). Cover and place in the oven. Don't bother checking it before three hours. Every hour after that, poke it with a knife. When the blade slides in and out, it's done. It will probably take about six hours.

Allow it to cool in the liquid, then strain. At this point I usually reduce the liquid to make a gravy or jus.

Refrigerate the beef. When it's cold, wrap it tightly in cling wrap and place it in the freezer for up to two months, or until Saturday's dinner.

Beef Mole and Pickled Celery

When I make mole sauce I use Hugh Fearnley-Whittingstall's recipe, from his great book *The River Cottage Meat Book*. I produce about 12 cups (3 L) and freeze it for later use. The first time I made mole I found it to be less work than everyone said it would be, but the second time I realized that it's still a lot of labour. Feel free to buy a jar of mole sauce or paste and loosen it with stock.

Wrapping the meat in a rich, fatty sauce means it needs something starchy and something acidic to balance it out. I like to tuck some caramelized parsnips, or just boiled potatoes, underneath. The pickled celery also prevents the dish from being one big mush.

2	celery stalks	2
1/2 cup	water	125 mL
1/8 cup	vinegar (rice wine, white wine, cider)	30 mL
1 1/2 tsp.	salt	7.5 mL
1 1/2 tsp.	sugar	7.5 mL
2	braised beef cheeks	2
1 tbsp.	fat (vegetable oil, but preferably duck fat)	15 mL
1/4 cup	commercially prepared mole (concentrated mole is sold at Latin grocers or in the ethnic food aisle of your supermarket)	60 mL
2 cups	chicken stock	500 mL
12	mini red potatoes, boiled and halved	12
1/4 cup	cilantro, chopped	60 mL

Peel the celery and julienne. In a small pot, boil the water, vinegar, salt, and sugar. Place in a container with the celery overnight to pickle. Refrigerate.

Slice the beef into six portions.

Heat the fat in a wide pan on medium heat. Add the mole, using a whisk to blend. Add the stock, and whisk until hot and smooth. Reduce the heat to low, add beef slices, and let them reheat in the sauce.

To serve, arrange the potatoes in the bottom of the dish. Top with the beef and pour the sauce over it. Put the pickled celery over the beef and sprinkle with cilantro.

Makes six servings.

Cheek Burgers

All we're doing here is substituting the braised meat for ground beef in a burger, but it's a startling substitution. The meat is already cooked. You're just going to add the finishing touch of crisping it in a pan.

2	braised beef cheeks	2
	salt to taste	
1 tsp.	vegetable oil	5 mL
4	processed cheese slices	4
4	Wonder Bread buns	4
	ketchup	
	mustard	
4	pickle slices	4

Slice the cheeks (chilled from fridge) in half, lengthwise. This should give you four oddly shaped but roughly patty-size discs that weigh about 4–6 oz. (113–170 g) each. Leave them at room temperature for thirty minutes.

Sprinkle each portion with salt. Heat the oil in a cast-iron pan on medium-high. When the oil sizzles, fry the cheeks on one side, untouched, until a crust forms, about two minutes. Flip and top with cheese. Fry until the cheese melts, about a minute.

Spread ketchup and mustard on the bottom half of the bun. Top with the cheek, pickles, and bun top.

Makes four servings.

CHAPTER FOUR

BEING ON TIME IS JUST BEING LATE FOR BEING early. Attempting to be ready at exactly the moment that our friends arrive is a fool's plan. Unless you're Captain America and can execute and improvise with split-second timing, give yourself the slack of thirty extra minutes.

Guests should be on time. A host needs to be early. Half an hour before your guests arrive, you should be showered, dressed, and ready. But that doesn't mean you're sitting around doing nothing (though you could and I often do).

This is my negotiable time. You know how we often wish there was an extra half-hour in every day, how there are just one or two tasks that we let slide because when it comes down to the crunch, there just isn't enough time? Well, that's what this half-hour is for. If anything went wrong in the kitchen, this is the time to fix it. Those emails or phone calls you ignored all afternoon because you prioritized readiness, because you refused to be distracted at every opportunity? Return them now.

I have a friend, a restaurateur, who goes home before service every night and takes a bath. This is the time for that. Imagine being so well prepared that you could be soaking in the tub before guests arrive. I like to recline on the sofa with a bourbon and, yes, return work emails.

The one thing I've found immeasurably helpful is inviting someone, or a couple, to arrive thirty minutes early. A pair of Early Birds has a number of benefits. First, it lights a fire under your bum to be ready. Second, there are now Early Birds if you need them. And sometimes I do. I have, on rare occasion, sent these people out to buy eggs, or asked someone to set the table or stir a sauce while I took a last-minute shower.

But the third and truly great thing that happens when you've scheduled guests to arrive during this pocket of time is that you get to ease into the dinner party, rather than diving into the deep end.

A couple of friends arrive, and these are probably your best friends, or maybe it's someone you haven't seen in a while. But either way, the Early Birds are people you're glad to gab with before everyone else gets there, so you can catch up on gossip, or maybe talk about something personal that you don't want to get into at the table. Pour them a drink and one for yourself.

These thirty minutes are like an airlock between the

two acts of a dinner party. This time helps separate the host from the labour of the prep time before the performance of showtime.

Put yourself into the social mood. Place your friend on door duty (but don't actually use the term "butler" or he or she will get resentful). As the guests arrive, you will want to spend time with each one. As we'll discuss in the next chapter, this is the critical stage of the evening. The doorbell can interrupt those initial, sometimes delicate moments. Having one of your Early Birds attend to that will allow you to multi-task at an important social juncture.

CHIPS AND GUAC

Nobody says no to a chip. This is a snack that you can be proud of, is simple to prepare, and can be served in moderation so guests don't fill themselves up.

While good guacamole only takes five minutes, it always impresses, probably because we're often subjected to such terrible guacamoles: garlicky, brown, flat. Make it fresh, cover it until serving to avoid oxidization, and for Odin's sake, don't add garlic. While this seems to be a mainstay of many guacamole recipes, I think that raw garlic makes avocados taste metallic and the whole dish has the vibrancy of an ashtray.

Ripe avocados, like a cab on a rainy night, are notoriously not there when you need them most. Toronto taquería Grand Electric pays extra to get avocados shipped from a warehouse, where they rotate the stock to have ripe ones always available. Shop for avocados a few days before your dinner. If they're rock hard, place them in a paper bag on the counter. If they're ripe, store them in the fridge until you're ready to use them.

Chips

2 lbs.	6 in. (15 cm) tortillas	1 kg
3 cups	vegetable oil	750 mL
1/2	a lime	1/2
	salt to taste	

In a large pot, heat oil to 350°F (175°C).

Slice the tortillas into quarters. In batches, fry the tortillas, stirring with slotted spoon to prevent overlapping. When golden, transfer to a stainless steel mixing bowl. Immediately toss with a small squeeze of lime and salt. Ideally, serve these warm, but you can always make them up to a few hours ahead of time.

Guacamole

1/8	Spanish onion, peeled and minced	1/8
1	jalapeno, stemmed, seeded and minced	1
2	ripe avocados	2
2	limes, juice of	2
	salt to taste	

In a large mixing bowl, combine the onion, jalapeno, and avocado flesh. Use a fork to mash the avocado until pulpy, but not puréed. Add lime juice and salt to taste. Refrigerate with cling wrap pressed into the surface to prevent discolouration.

Serves four.

CHAPTER FIVE

THIS IS WHAT YOU'VE BEEN TRAINING FOR.

When you open that door, it's going to be lights, camera, action. For about fifteen minutes, your behaviour will cue everyone else. During prep or dinner you can check your notes. But for this opening act, you need to be off script because there will be people arriving, in need of warm greetings, drinks, and introductions.

They haven't been labouring over menus. They may not understand the intricacies of why you think they'll like the other guests. They may not know where the bathroom is. They need direction from you, and they need to know that you're thinking of them and of their comfort. They need to know it right away, or they will begin to suspect that you do not have their best interests at heart, that the evening ahead may be less than delightful.

So this is when it's important to show the most confidence. Do you think, on the first day of shooting, Alfred Hitchcock asked his crew, "Where do you think we should put the cameras?"

THE DOOR

 Hosting is a performance. That doesn't mean you're being a phony, but there is, by necessity, some theatricality to the evening. When the doorbell rings, it's showtime. By spending the last thirty or even ten minutes with the Early Birds, you should be eased into character, rather than having the curtain suddenly raised while you're still in makeup.

The average dinner party has a pace, a flow, that we settle into once people have found their places and been served some food and wine. The first fifteen minutes are the most important fifteen minutes of the evening and can make or break the night.

My apartment is on the third floor. This means running down the stairs when I hear the doorbell, slowly making my way back up with my guests, pausing as they remove their shoes on the second-floor landing, then, just as I've taken their coats, running back downstairs as the bell rings again.

The Early Birds — the friends you've been relaxing with for the last little while — will now become Helping

Hands, integral players in the next act. These characters perform three critical roles:

1. Just being present. A lot of guests, on arrival, ask, "Are we the first ones here?" Often they ask this with an implied anxiety, as if there were something dreadful to being on time, or the idea of a one-on-one conversation is too much pressure. Just seeing that someone else is already there will put them at ease.

2. Depending on how many guests you're expecting and whether or not you have stairs between you and the front door, these fifteen minutes can be a whirlwind. The doors, coats, introductions, and drinks can come so fast that a host starts to feel like Lucy in the chocolate factory, with a conveyor belt of greetings coming at her. The Helping Hands need little prodding. Just a simple, "Could you ... ?" and they're off to get the door. Many guests, once they're regulars, start doing this without being prompted.

3. Ask an audience member for improv suggestions and they draw a blank. But once the crowd starts shouting out "Iceland! Pirates! Singles Bingo!" everyone wants in on the action. The same thing goes for conversation. When guests start arriving and find that there is already a couple in the living room arguing away over municipal politics, traffic, whether *Tron* has any value beyond nostalgia for eighties nerd children, they'll be in the mood to talk, too. Conversation can be a highway. You are a merging lane.

When the doorbell rings, remember that different people need different amounts of attention. You are always happy to see your close friends, but those you haven't met before — spouses of friends, partners, associates — need more of the host's attention. They are in a new environment, with new people. They need to feel welcome and engaged. Take their coats ahead of others. Get them a drink first. If George's wife is uncomfortable, then George is uncomfortable. Put her at ease. When she is seated, with a glass of wine in her hand, smiling, you will see the ripple of relaxation spread outward.

A LATENESS TIMETABLE

 While it is to a host's advantage to be ready thirty minutes before dinner, a guest should arrive on time, and no more than ten minutes early.

A friend told me he once had guests show up thirty minutes early. He sent them away, and told them to come back in half an hour. He is my hero. The host is not expected to be actually ready half an hour ahead of schedule. It can throw someone totally off of their game to suddenly have to socialize when there are still last-minute tasks to be done.

Lateness is also rude, but it is acceptable, understandable, and forgivable if tardy people take responsibility for their behaviour. If you believe you will arrive late, let your host know as soon as possible. If dinner is for 7:00, calling at 7:15 to say you are going to be late is not only factually inaccurate, but grounds for dismissal. Calling at 6:45 can buy you all the time in the world.

If you're not certain just how serious the infraction is, consult this handy tardiness timetable:

FIVE TO TEN MINUTES EARLY = Acceptable

PUNCTUALITY = Ideal

FIVE MINUTES LATE = The discrepancy between two watches, not worth mentioning

TEN MINUTES LATE = A trifle, easily the result of a missed train, slow elevator, or difficulty in finding a parking spot

FIFTEEN MINUTES LATE = Worth a minor "I'm sorry," which will be forgotten just as quickly

TWENTY MINUTES = You should have called ahead to announce your impending lateness; if not, a light apology is needed

TWENTY-FIVE MINUTES = An apology and explanation are needed

THIRTY MINUTES = An apology and explanation are needed; expect your host to be upset, though he or she should not show it; try to make up for it later with a gift, or take your friend to lunch

A Chilean guest once told me that none of this counts in her home country, that in Chile it would be rude to show up on time, so if you are in Chile, disregard this.

Lateness puts hosts in an awkward position. Once a guest is twenty minutes late without calling, you as a host are not happy about it. However, whether friends are unconscionably early or late, do not show your annoyance. You are still a host, and a host must occasionally swallow certain indignities in aid of the guests' enjoyment. This goes for corked wine, spilled wine, spilled milk, tardy guests, dishes that didn't turn out how you expected, being asked "When are you going to get married? When are you going to have children?", broken glasses, muddy shoes, stinky feet, cigarette breath, re-regifted wine, cutoff shorts, a guest who spoils the season finale of a show you haven't watched yet, etc.

If you don't like the way a guest behaves, you can always tell the person later, or simply not invite him or her again, but don't spoil everyone else's time by having it out at the table. If you call out someone's bad behaviour in front of others, it will only make everyone uncomfortable. The needs of the many must come before the one or the few.

THE FIRST DRINK

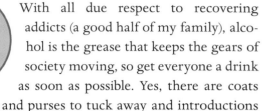 With all due respect to recovering addicts (a good half of my family), alcohol is the grease that keeps the gears of society moving, so get everyone a drink as soon as possible. Yes, there are coats and purses to tuck away and introductions to make. But don't be ambushed by the detour of putting flowers in a vase. Ask someone else to do that.

The worst thing a host can do at this point is to be too busy to pour drinks. Many times when I have been among the guests at a dinner party, the host has simply left us alone while he or she fiddled with the stove, chopped garlic, or emailed questions about a recipe. Once I arrived at a dinner to find the host insisting that everyone join him in the kitchen while he peeled potatoes. Fine, I said, so long as I get to drink while you do it.

We spent all that time planning and prepping so that when our guests arrive, we can look after their needs, rather than our own.

The easiest thing is to get them a drink without asking if they want one. Try, "What can I get you to drink?" Do not ask, "Can I get you a drink?" Of course you can. Maybe things work differently in the real world, but in Canada, people are so deferential and polite that they'll pass up the offer of a drink. Balderdash. Everyone wants a drink of some sort.

The usual response from guests is, "What are you drinking?" It's a good idea to have a bottle of wine already open, as they'll be less likely to refuse. Let them know

THE SHOE DILEMMA

Shoes on or off? This is up to the host. In my home, I ask people to take their shoes off only if it's raining or snowing, otherwise I like my guests to have the dignity of wearing their shoes, which probably go with their outfit. But I've got floors that are easy to sweep and mop. If you've got carpeting, that's a different story. To many North Americans, it would be unthinkable to ask guests to remove their shoes. In Japan it would be inconceivable to enter a house wearing outside shoes. Guests, respect your hosts' shoe rules.

If guests are expected to remove their shoes, have a place for it. Respect the footwear. Don't let shoes be piled on top of each other.

If a guest is truly opposed to removing shoes, he or she will bring slippers. Yes, I have had guests do this and it is basically the cutest thing ever. Everyone makes fun of them a bit and then says, "Why didn't I think of that?" But don't linger on it. Consider that this person may be a germaphobe or may suffer from an uncontrollable foot odour problem.

you've got a red and a white open. There are people who think that opening a bottle is tantamount to rewriting a living will.

If guests bring you cold beer, that probably means they like to drink beer, so offer them one. Too many people think that, as grown-ups, they're expected to drink wine even if they don't like it.

Then there are the guests who will ask for a cocktail. It's usually something basic, a vodka tonic or a rye and ginger. If you've got the ingredients, make it. If not, don't apologize. Just suggest something else. If you've got the ingredients but don't want to make it or are too busy, pretend that you don't have the ingredients.

In my experience, the type of person who exclusively drinks vodka tonics is likely suffering from a dash of alcoholism and a pinch of OCD, so he or she has probably brought the ingredients. If people ask for water, do not chastise them for being a baby. It could be hot outside. They may have cycled over. They could be nursing a hangover. Whatever the reason, don't ask. Just get them a glass of water.

And then there are recovering addicts, devout Muslims, pregnant women, and other sorts of non-drinkers. Ideally, this should have come up when you asked about food restrictions. Most people don't volunteer this information. They don't like having to explain themselves and they don't like the possibility of being put on the disabled list for being non-drinkers. They have every right to feel this way.

I've had guests avoid telling me that they don't drink, just as I've had guests do the same with vegetarianism or gluten allergies. They're trying not to stand out, but in thinking that they'll "just eat around it," they are making things more awkward. If you know in advance, you can cater to their needs.

If you know that a guest is a non-drinker, find out what he or she likes to drink — a favourite juice or soda. Keep some basics on hand. Recovering alcoholics tend to maintain their loyalty to club soda and ginger ale. And always stock a bit of carbonated water, even if you don't like the stuff.

But whatever they're drinking, get them something. Not only can people use a little lubrication, they need something in their hand. They are often in a strange environment and sometimes a prop as simple as a glass of wine or whisky, or even water, can be enough to settle them.

If you are standing, your guests will stand. Most guests won't sit until they're told to or given a visual cue. Sitting down and suggesting, "Make yourselves comfortable" is more persuasive than bluntly saying, "Have a seat." Some hosts, depending on the space or the amount of people, want that standing/mingling atmosphere. It's up to you, but it's important that you decide where you want guests to be. Don't expect eight people to sit down in your living room if there are only enough seats for six.

THE INTRODUCTIONS

If you are hosting a dinner for besties, where everyone knows and likes each other, skip this step, otherwise you may need to make some introductions.

A grown-up knows how to enter a room of strangers, handshake extended. You see this at weddings. There's always that guy who walks right up, shakes your hand, and tells you not only his name but his association to the bride or groom. "Hey, I'm Jackie. I'm Estelle's cousin from Milwaukee. I introduced her to Morty. We were undergrads together. Used to call him T-Bone. He's got a scar on his left thigh and can't swing a nine iron." These people are usually in sales.

If you see people introducing themselves and looking comfortable, stand back. Let the adults talk. But some people are shy. Some people are young. Some people have terrible memories for names.

At this moment, friends who know each other well will greet one another with hugs and exclamations. Those who don't know everyone may find themselves outsiders, pushed aside, waiting to be introduced. Be on the ball here. Watch for it, and pounce.

If you see that new person standing alone for more than five seconds, slide in between the Best Friends Gang. "Carol," you interrupt in a commanding voice, "do you know Dr. Van Nostrand? He cured my Seborrheic dermatitis."

You're not looking to hand anyone the microphone. No one wants to enter a room of strangers and be expected to take a position on foreign policy.

What you want is to get people talking — about anything — and hopefully to eliminate that wretched non sequitur, "So how do you two know each other?" That's one of those perfectly reasonable questions that is nevertheless symbolic of dead air. There is nothing wrong with talking about the weather. Maybe it was particularly hot or cold or wet or dry. Sometimes when we discuss the weather, what we are really doing is agreeing to converse, agreeing that we share some common experience, and out of that comes something more meaningful.

This is your chance to introduce new characters, possibly with the nature of your association. It's not about formality, like the servants of British aristocracy announcing guests as they enter, "Sir William of Brooklyn!" It's about creating a dialogue, providing discussion merging ramps, telling your own story, if necessary, to jog the conversation of others, before you leave them alone. One should not babble like a drive-time radio host, but gently coax interaction from people, perhaps by relating a story with plenty of holes in it, openings for guests to ask questions or take things in a different direction.

A teacher once told me that if you can get a student to talk within the first five minutes of class, he or she is more likely to participate during the rest of the class. It's the same for dinner guests. When you're a host, you never need an excuse to walk away, but get a conversation started first.

And, most important, have faith. Not only can things start off awkwardly, they usually do. I've experienced this many times. People come in, they meet, and behind their eyes is a performance of a one-act play titled *This Is Going to Be Awful*. When things aren't immediately smooth, some people panic. The bad host will be impatient, demanding anecdotes from their guests. "Mike, tell that story you were telling me earlier. It's hilarious." If Mike is hilarious, he's going to be hilarious. All you will communicate with behaviour like this is that you are not confident, and your guests will not be confident in you.

My advice for you, as hosts, is to have faith. In my experience, things smooth out 100 percent of the time. People find shared ground and discover that they have more in common than they thought, which usually happens within ten minutes. Take a deep breath and carry on.

PUNCH

A cocktail is a sophisticated way to start any evening. But mixing a good drink requires attention — measuring ingredients, stirring, tasting, icing— and at an evening's critical beginning, your attention is needed elsewhere.

If you really want to serve a cocktail, this is what punch is for. Punch has many meanings. For our purposes, it is a cocktail that can be mixed and chilled in advance, presented in a large vessel, allowing guests to serve themselves.

My friend Jen Agg is a restaurateuroperating several establishments under the Black Hoof banner. Not a month goes by without some magazine writing a profile about her cocktail-making skills, but she doesn't do things the easy way. Here is her "basic" recipe for punch.

Punch Recipe

1	lemon, zest of	1
1	orange, zest of	1
2 oz.	gin	60 mL
3 oz.	rum	80 mL
2 oz.	spiced rum	60 mL
2	sprigs of mint	2
1 oz.	Crème de Cassis (or simple syrup, fruit purée, maple syrup)	30 mL
4 oz.	ginger ale	125 mL
4 oz.	club soda	125 mL
2 oz.	lemon juice	60 mL
2 oz.	lime juice	60 mL
4 oz.	orange juice	125 mL
4 oz.	pink grapefruit juice	125 mL
5 dashes	Peychaud's bitters	5 dashes
6 oz.	sparkling wine	175 mL

In a 32 oz. (1 L) Mason jar, combine the lemon and orange zest with the gin, rum, and spiced rum. Let it sit for one to three days. Strain.

It's better if you can do this earlier in the day to let the flavours mingle.

Have all ingredients chilled to start.

Rub the inside of the jar with one mint sprig. Pour the liquors back in. Add the Crème de Cassis, ginger ale, club soda, lemon, lime, orange, and pink grapefruit juices. Stir.

To finish, add the bitters and sparkling wine. Stir and top with fresh mint.

Serve in the jar. Or, if you're multiplying the recipe, fill a large bowl with ice. Place the punch in a smaller bowl and mount on the ice. Put out a ladle and cups and let your guests figure it out.

Once you've gotten the hang of this, you can experiment with the ingredients, so long as you stick to the ratios. "What you could do with this recipe," explains Jen, "is take out the mint or the spiced rum or have all gin and no rum or you could switch out the citrus. You could just do lemon and orange. You can take anything out so long as you replace it with something that adds the same character."

Serves four.

CHAPTER SIX

SOON, AS THE HOST, WE MUST DISENGAGE FROM the group. The guests are all in place. They're drinking. They're talking. And while you've just gone through the toughest fifteen minutes of the whole evening, at some point you need to go to the kitchen and put dinner on the table.

I try to steal away with the quiet grace of Santa Claus or a ninja or (spoiler alert) your parents when they pretended to be Santa, furtively slipping candy and toys into your Christmas stocking. The way not to do it is like my father, bluntly demanding that we change the channel because the Cosbys were celebrating Christmas.

Sneak away quietly or run the risk of breaking the spell

you've cast, the warm bubble of fresh conversation that should envelop your friends while you scurry to your labour. If you are not quiet, you will hear …

THE MEDDLERS

"Is there anything I can do to help?" This question is a red flag that you need to be prepared for. It can mean one of three things.

1. The guest loves to cook or help.

2. The guest feels a sense of responsibility, or guilt that you're working away in the kitchen while he or she is relaxing.

3. The guest is nervous and, lacking the ability to make conversation with new people, wants to be busy in the kitchen.

There's nothing wrong with any of these. But know in advance if you do need or want help with anything. If you've prepared this feast for your friends, you probably don't need some last-minute meddler getting in your way in the kitchen. Your job — making introductions and pouring the drinks — is to break the evening's ice for them. And you've retreated to the kitchen only when you see that people are happily engaged with each other. But if you think that a guest is asking because they feel uncomfortable, say no, you don't need any help, but you'd love some company in the kitchen.

You've just got to tell would-be helpers where to stand. There are people who, like a golden retriever, will position themselves at the room's nexus or bottleneck. Feel free to direct them: "I need you to stand there and not move." Guests need to know that the kitchen is a workplace and that they should not get in the way. They should find the corner of the room that is the least used and stand there, not pace back and forth to stay close to the cook. The cook is working and needs room to move around — room to reach the bowls in the top cupboard and the whisk in the third drawer on the right.

Hanging out in the kitchen can be fun, but if as a guest you notice that your host has become flustered, is unable to communicate, keeps looking at a printed recipe, is doing double-takes, pick up on these as cues that they are not able to talk and cook at the same time. Many would like to but cannot. Also, if you're having a nice, cozy time in the kitchen but then others join you, watch to see if your host's posture and tone changes, if they are now less able to cook. Be the team leader — "We should all get out of the kitchen and let Helen do her thing."

As a host, you might consider leaving some simple tasks for guests to do, such as putting out napkins or opening wine. But this is transparently busy work, the sort we use to distract an overly energetic child. Be more strategic — this is your chance to make a tiny investment that will reap large dividends. "I'm all set now," you tell your friend, "but maybe in between courses you could help with the dishes?" Believe me, you'll be cashing that IOU.

There are many labours during the meal. Food must be cooked, wine and water poured, dishes cleared and washed, lighting and music adjusted. Once you've hosted enough times, it becomes less of a performance filled with checklists and stopwatches and more of a ship of which you are captain, gently steering the conversation whenever it gets off course, keeping the engine running with food and the gears oiled with alcohol.

The guests are your passengers and your crew (yes, I've grown as tired of this metaphor as you have). During the meal, take up your friends' offers of assistance. There may be some who wouldn't feel as if they'd participated if they didn't wash a plate or pour a drink.

However, some people do not want to lift a finger as guests, nor should they have to. That's what makes this country great. It is their right and I support them in this. You can expect their spouse to nag them for not helping. This is always humorous to watch, but do not nag a guest.

THE SNACK

Hungry people should be fed. If you've invited friends to your house to eat, there is a reasonable expectation that they will arrive hungry. And, in turn, they have a reasonable expectation that you will feed them in a timely manner. These two events need to synchronize a little — your guests should not be without food for too long.

My solution to this is to get dinner started without too

much preamble. I aim to have the first course on the table within half an hour of guests arriving.

The other solution is to serve something before dinner. This could be as simple as leaving bowls of nuts and dried fruits on the table where you're having your drinks, just something for idle hands and nibblers. It could be a more substantial snack of bread and cheese. Or you might get really involved and do passed hors d'oeuvres of hot food.

I don't like any of these. Not that I don't enjoy being served or being fed, but my problem with the passed hors d'oeuvres is that they inevitably requires too much last-minute labour on the part of the host. Blinis topped with caviar and crème fraîche are a wonderful two-bite start to the evening. However, at the moment when ice is still being broken, the host shouldn't be at the stove, flipping blinis or gingerly dolloping each one with garnish. And walking around with a serving plate is just too precious for me.

Of course that depends on your home and the type of tone you're trying to set. If I had the floor space and I was celebrating my wife's tenure by hosting the dean and the treasurer of the endowment board, yes, passed hors d'oeuvres would be in order.

But in my home, if there's going to be any type of pre-dinner snack, I prefer it to be something that can be laid out on the coffee table. The casualness of reaching for a slice of prosciutto or deciding how big a wedge to carve off of a brick of Taleggio is more in keeping with the informal tone we want our guests to feel.

My concern is with giving guests too much food before dinner. Just as planning a final course with a negotiable

amount of starch can help to adjust for the remaining appetites at the end of the evening, providing guests with too
much at the beginning can demolish those appetites.

If they arrive hungry and you provide them with a
loaf of bread you've bought or a big bag of chips in a bowl,
they're going to eat it all, particularly if you keep them
waiting too long for dinner. Offering a large amount of
starch before supper, without portioning it, is a recipe for
ruining appetites. And if you put out too small an amount,
it looks chintzy. Better to get dinner on the table quickly.

Caveat: If you fry your own chips or bake your own
bread, feel free to start with this. But tell people about the
effort so they appreciate it.

THE SEATING AND THE SEATS

Whether you're serving a six-course meal
or a big shared feast, at some point you
have to start eating. Guests sometimes
get comfortable with cocktails on the
sofa, and are too entrenched in conversation to be easily corralled. Without being a
dictator, get your guests to the dinner table.

If guests are in the living room, you might think that
taking a seat at the dining table would send a message, but
if they're having a good time — and they should be — they
won't want to move, so you're going to have to motivate
them. You can do this with the carrot or the stick.

The carrot is to bring out a dish that you're serving,
steam billowing, filling the room with the perfume of its

THE STARTING LINE

It's not always easy to know when to fire the starting pistol for dinner. You've got to read the crowd. One time I had an acupuncturist as a guest. She poked needles into everyone's head and hands, and I think that most of us could have sat there for a long time, relaxing, but eventually, I had to get my pork loin back in the oven.

Another guest who brought his work to dinner was the manager of the city's food inspection agency. I asked him to bring his kit and wanted to do the inspection pre-dinner (like a restaurant, it's cleaner at 5 p.m. than at 11 p.m.). But I also figured I'd get a more generous review after the meal. Marked on "the Chinatown curve," I passed.

The director of a ballet school, appointed to be the mayor's arts adviser, was so unable to speak candidly for political reasons that we quickly reached a conversational stalemate and dinner needed to be the focus of the evening.

Another awkward evening was a dinner for a group of home brewers. I figured that since they all knew each other and hung out regularly, they would slide right into conversation, but until they reached their third beer, not one of them was talkative. So even though I just had to run to the stove and reheat the ribs I'd smoked that day, they needed a long babysitting until they could safely be left alone.

I've hosted the occasional brunch. Even if people are coming over at noon, assume that they are ravenous. They have no time for small pre-meal bites. You've got to get them fed and soon.

So try to get food on the table within a half-hour. Rather than using a stopwatch, be flexible and read your guests' moods and appetites.

spices. As the warm food catches everyone's attention, you ask, "Would you join me at the dining table?" And your guests should follow you, Pied Piper style.

But maybe your first course doesn't lend itself to this type of cheap theatrics. Maybe it's too heavy or too hot. Maybe it's soup.

The stick is to go into the living room and declare, "Boy, you better get your ass to the dining table," or "Would everyone please take a seat at the dinner table?" Be authoritative and make eye contact with at least one person until he or she gets up. Beware the group mentality. If you speak to the group without singling anyone out and then leave the room before anyone rises, the whole pack might just sit there.

The Seats

For an intimate dinner party, there should not be assigned seating. Even if you don't have formal seating assignments, guests will wait to be told. If you see them hovering, let them know, "Please sit wherever you would like."

In some strange vestige of our patriarchal past (I hope it's the past), guests are hesitant to take a seat at the head of the table. Unless you are royalty or a CEO, there is nothing special about the ends of the table. If anything, they are the worst seats because they are the dead ends of conversation, where you have the fewest options of whom to talk to.

As a host, I usually take the end of the table to let others converse more freely. Sit in the middle only if you feel you're needed to help facilitate conversation. If there is a guest who will assist you between courses — if he or she has specifically volunteered — have the person seated in a position where he or she can see you in the kitchen, or at least the entrance to the kitchen. If the guest's back is turned to you, he or she will quickly lose interest in being of assistance.

TOMATOES

When tomatoes are in season, they should be served with a minimum of manipulation. Cold gazpacho soup and a well-made tomato sandwich are two great ways to present the flavour of a tomato.

Gazpacho

Chopping tomatoes will make lumpy gazpacho. Puréeing them in a food processor or blender will make it frothy. After much experimentation and many bad directions, I discovered the secret of gazpacho in Paul Bertolli's book *Cooking by Hand*. It is easy, but depends on tools. You will need a Kitchen Aid-style mixer and a food mill (aka a ricer). The slow paddle of a mixer will thoroughly separate the liquid from solid without whipping air into it.

12	tomatoes, cored and roughly chopped	12
1	shallot, peeled and finely diced	1
1/4	zucchini, finely diced	1/4
1	yellow bell pepper, finely diced	1
1/4	bird's eye chili, minced	1/4
1 tsp.	red wine vinegar	5 mL
	salt	

Place the freshest, most flavourful tomatoes you can find (sniff them at the core, and if they smell more like fridge than tomato, pass on them) in the bowl of a kitchen mixer. Use the paddle attachment on a low speed until the tomatoes are pulped. Be patient. This may take ten minutes. Pour the mixture into the ricer with a bowl placed underneath. The liquid is what we'll use for gazpacho, but reserve the skins. You can always toss those into a sauce.

Add the remaining ingredients to the tomato liquid. Season to taste. Store at room temperature and serve the same day.

Serves four.

Tomato Sandwiches

You may think a tomato sandwich too lowly to serve to guests. But so long as it's not the main course, it will be welcome. Serve it with the soup as a representation of an ingredient in its prime.

Here are some tips for making it great.

Making your own mayonnaise will elevate the dish in both taste and stature. When I was a kid, we didn't really keep mayo in our house, so I didn't discover the glory of a tomato sandwich until I was older. Still, I grew up with challah and prefer it for most of my sandwiches. A sourdough also will be good, as long as it's a bread with more body and less crust.

Toast the bread. Spread a little mustard on the top slice and lots of tarragon mayonnaise on the bottom. Instead of thin layers of tomatoes (which will result in the tomato squeezing out of the sandwich), slice them as thick as the bread and lay them out without overlapping. Sprinkle with salt and pepper. Serve.

For the tarragon mayonnaise

1	egg yolk	1
1 tsp.	Dijon mustard	5 mL
1/2 tsp.	lemon juice	2.5 mL
1 1/2 cups	olive oil	375 mL
	salt to taste	
1 bunch	tarragon leaves	1 bunch
1/2 tsp.	lime juice	2.5 mL

Place the egg yolk, Dijon mustard, and lemon juice in a mixing bowl with a splash of water. Whisk and slowly drizzle 1 cup (250 mL) of olive oil in as thin a stream as possible. When it emulsifies into a glossy, thick mayo, transfer it to a bowl and season to taste with salt.

In a blender, purée the tarragon with the remaining oil and lime juice. Season with salt and fold into the mayo.

It'll keep in the fridge for a week. Use cling wrap inside the container to prevent discolouration.

If the mayo breaks (separates and stays thin), start with another yolk, slowly adding the first broken batch back into the mix.

CHAPTER SEVEN

YOU HAVE SUCCESSFULLY PASSED THOSE CRITI-
cal first fifteen minutes. Your guests have been
lulled into a state of relaxation, your gentle coaxing with wine and conversation allowing them to believe
that this is all just happening without some greater power
steering its course. But when the time comes to serve
food, you must assert your authority as the warden of this
food prison. In addition to expressing confidence — for
who will follow a leader who does not believe in himself
or herself? — it is important to not be over-prepared or
under-prepared. Also, do not use the term "food prison" at
the dinner table. (Or in a book about dinner parties).

GETTING STARTED

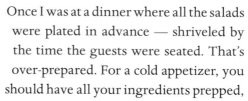

Once I was at a dinner where all the salads were plated in advance — shriveled by the time the guests were seated. That's over-prepared. For a cold appetizer, you should have all your ingredients prepped, but not assembled. At another dinner, the guests were seated and then told that the soup would take just a while to warm up. Soup, as opposed to a slice of seared foie gras or a poached egg, is a pretty forgiving hot appetizer. If your first course is soup, bring it to a boil, cover it and turn off the heat, and then tell people dinner's ready. These are details to have considered in the planning stage.

Both of these seem like basic "shoes go over socks, not the other way around" common sense. But some people get flustered around food and lose their sense of how long things take. If you need a hand in cooking or plating, or just want to accept the offer, ask the Helping Hand before they sit down again and get wrapped up in another conversation.

"In about five minutes, I'm going to need you to help me plate," you say. Or, "Can I put you in charge of making sure everyone's water glass is full?" Then, at the moment you need their assistance, tap them lightly on the elbow. They'll know what to do.

Bring the Helping Hand into the kitchen and give them clear instructions. If you are running around like a headless chicken, it is unlikely that the Helping Hand will understand your directions to "put a bit of lentils on each plate." Be precise. How much lentils, one spoonful or two? In the centre of the plate or on the side? If they are helping you plate a row of six dishes, do one first to demonstrate exactly how you want it to look.

If you are changing cutlery in between courses, make sure each guest has what he or she needs before being served. You don't want your well-timed dish to get cold as you fumble for forks.

If you are serving family style, you may expect guests to start digging in as soon as food hits the table. But as you return from the kitchen with each new dish, you'll see that guests are still waiting patiently, the food untouched. As children, we may have grabbed for sustenance as soon as the food arrived, without waiting for our mothers or fathers to sit down. But our guests will not start eating until the host is seated.

Pay special attention to this, you hosts who are too full of performance anxiety to be seated. I was taught that hot food is meant to be eaten hot. So if your guests appear too socially inhibited to start before you sit down, even after your insistence, you may need to be seated, just to get the ball rolling. In this situation, sometimes I'll sit down and begin to put food on my plate or eat, just long enough to get others started. It's like when you have to suck a bit of gas from a car tank before siphoning it into a bottle.

You will likely need to introduce the food, but the table may have an impenetrable dialogue you don't want to interrupt. Too bad for them. You made this soup. They should hear what it is and eat it before it gets cold. Sometimes people will stop their conversation when they see food, but don't depend on that.

Here's a trick. While serving a dish, get in between two people who are talking. I mean physically in between. In the second when they pause, say, "I don't want to interrupt, so I'll just tell you that you're having a smoked eggplant soup." This probably will interrupt things, but conversations branch in so many directions. It is everyone's right, but primarily the host's, to make those digressions.

If you do not introduce a dish but simply start eating, others will eat. When there is a pause, someone will comment on it, hopefully with a flattering sincerity, and ask, "What are we eating?" Some hosts like to make a big event about this, but that can backfire if your dish doesn't live up to the hype you've just given it. Talking too much about a dish before it's eaten can build undue expectations. Guests will hunker down with nachos as if they were taking an exam, feeling the need to form some clever summation, wasting time on pith when they should be enjoying melted cheese.

It's pretty embarrassing to clink a fork against a wineglass, demand the floor, and address everyone as "ladies and gentleman," only to oversell a roast beef that you've burned. I once had a host include salt and pepper in his explanation of his dish. Please err on the side of brevity. Do not list every last ingredient down to the microscopic level. We know that the dish contains both protons and electrons.

If you are serving confit lamb shoulder with a parsnip purée, jus, and whisky-soaked apricots, try introducing it as "lamb, parsnip, and apricot." This gives your guests the opportunity to discover the depth of flavours and textures on their own, and, if they desire, to ask questions about how it was made.

TECHNOLOGY AT THE TABLE

Some guests will ask for a phone charger, terrified that they'll miss a text from a friend who is glued to tonight's episode of *America's Somethingest Something*. Some people plop their phone down next to the plate, as if it were part of the cutlery set. Others are aghast if anyone looks at their phone or if it rings, even in silent mode.

There's no definitively final word on cellphone use at dinner other than the obvious conclusion that it's rude. At my table, I don't mind phones for the purpose of settling disputes, but other than as a pocket-sized encyclopedia, I don't want to see one in use.

The ways that we interact with technology have changed. We share information differently than we used to. Let's be honest about that. Most people do not own dictionaries or encyclopedias anymore. Settling a bet by looking up facts is a perfectly good use for a smartphone.

However, I had a pair of dinner guests who introduced me to the Challenge of Three. If a fact is disputed at the dinner table, make three attempts to solve it before using Google. Call a friend, look it up in a book (gasp), or use deductive reasoning. I know this sounds like rubbing two sticks together to make fire, but when you avoid the shortcut of reaching directly for the easy answer, you'll find yourself connecting with people in a more active, meaningful way. The dudes who suggested this rule were engineers. So they did have an obsessive interest in problem solving.

The only people allowed to put their phones on the table are doctors who are on call. And parents with children under ten month old. Everyone else should keep it in their pants. There are very few emergencies in this life. Most of them can wait for an hour. A lot of parents like to claim their need to be available to the babysitter as an excuse to keep checking their phones, but I've seen these same people pretend to check in with the sitter and then tell me who's winning the hockey game.

Our dinner mates should not have to compete with a glowing screen for anyone's attention. Smartphones are just the current example of a recurring conflict. This includes phones, televisions, computers, and whatever else humanity is likely to create, whatever new devices will make our lives easier but will cause us to miss out on more basic human experiences. I've accepted that life has become more digital and less personal, but when we are gathered with friends, we take a break from the daily world of the short attention span where every movie ever made becomes boring because we can download another one in five minutes.

We need not be distracted by every hyperlink that pops into our head. Just because you saw a funny video on the Internet doesn't mean that everyone at the table needs to see it. If you cannot tell the story without displaying the video, perhaps it's not worth telling.

And even if others do want to see it, consider how it affects the evening.

When a group is sitting across from each other, making eye contact, listening, and arguing, people are active. When you insist on showing everyone something on your phone – a cat that looks like Hitler, your child's first steps, a parody of the pop culture thing you've been talking about – you're asking them to switch into the passive mode and then jump back into the social one. Think about how people behave in a movie theatre after the lights come back on. They're dazed, blinking, unresponsive. They need a walk to the parking lot to jog their conversational muscles.

At all costs, prevent your guests from staring at a glowing screen. If you have a friend who is a particularly bad offender, you are within your rights to confiscate the device at the beginning of the evening.

THE PRESENTATION

Yes, good food is more important than good-looking food, but this isn't a cafeteria. Even simple food — a bowl of soup or a plate of sliced steak with potatoes — deserves to be served with respect.

Soups need garnishes. And it need not be a butter-poached lobster tail (though no one would complain about that). Something as simple as a sprinkling of crushed nuts, seeds, or quinoa with a drizzle of olive oil can make a huge difference.

Plates should be clean. If a plate has a rim, that is where the food stops. Roll up a cloth, wrap it in elastic bands and wet it. Use the roll to wipe sauce spills from the rims of plates before serving them. Drips on the plate's edge — a natural result of transferring, say, freshly sliced pieces of rare beef from the cutting board — look messy. No one would ever remark on it, the way that no one would complain about an A grade. But if an A+ can be had by taking a second to wipe the plate, why not go for the bonus marks? Most guests wouldn't even register messy plates, at least on a conscious level. But cleanliness makes an impression.

If, while you're carrying plates to the table, food falls over or sauces slide, let it go. Yes, in a high-end restaurant, if the chef's stack of polenta fries topples, servers will return to the kitchen for a re-plate. At home, this is a step too far. Going back to your kitchen to re-plate food will make it look like you're trying way too hard. If I make a mess on the way to the table, or if I notice at the last minute that a plate is chipped, then that's the plate that I serve to myself.

Plate Design

How the food will look is something you considered back in the planning stage (see Chapter Two). If you've sketched out your meal, snap it on the fridge with magnets. Consult your drawings before each course, so that you don't forget key ingredients.

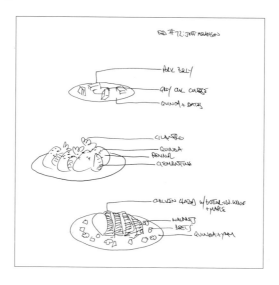

Stay away from square plates. A square is a fine shape, perfectly suited to the spaces on a tic-tac-toe board, Japanese watermelons, or, in a forgotten era, televisions. Even if objects within that space are not consciously placed in one of four quadrants, something about a square frame for this purpose feels off. If this book were a square, it would fail to impart the serious tone of its contents. Stick with circles and rectangles. When assembling a dish, try to focus your food in the centre. Don't worry so much about elements overlapping. It will look cleaner and more appetizing when it's clustered, rather than spread out. It will also retain heat better.

On the subject of volume, try to stick to your plan. It's to your advantage to make too much of everything, but not to dole it all out. Whether it's tomato sauce on spaghetti or jus on lamb, there can be too much of a good thing. The mistake that a lot of people make is to distribute what they have proportionately, rather than execute the plate design from their plans. No one does this on purpose. It's more like that time you tried to even out your sideburns and ended up bald. What happens is that the cook portions the food out, then sees how much is left, and proceeds to dump sauce on all the plates to use it up. Only after it's done does the cook look at the soupy mess and realize that it isn't what they intended.

If there is supposed to be a streak of jus next to the slices of lamb, make that streak on each plate even if you have enough jus for two, or three, or four tablespoons. If people rave about the sauce, serve them more. It'll be a nice surprise that you have more in the pot.

Now, about those streaks. Chefs have a number of tools in specific shapes for getting food onto the plates: squeeze bottles, piping bags, metal moulds, stencils. But they also have technique that, like any artist, they've perfected over years of repetition and experimentation. Their work cannot be replicated simply by buying their tools any more than purchasing a basketball will enable you to dunk. Nor should this be your goal.

You want to brush a perfect rectangle of your cumin/raisin purée on the bottom of the plate? For the lamb? Where do you think you are? Is there a camera crew behind you? Are your guests paying $150 each? No. You are at home. And to be at home, with your friends, and think it is a good use of your time to hunch over the kitchen counter painting sauce onto a plate with a stencil and brush is to misunderstand the very nature of the dinner party.

Those streaks, where the sauce is a sort of fat blob at one end, and trails off to nothingness as it rides the curve of the plate, are literally all in the wrist. I can write the directions plainly enough: tip a spoonful of sauce to the plate and, in one smooth motion, drag it across the surface, lifting up at the end. But those are just words and the method is all about motion, having a confident, relaxed wrist, and having repeated the gesture a hundred times. Speed is important. Your lines must be assured and fluid. Slowly dragging the tip of the bottle or spoon against the plate will result in a bumpy, uneven line. You must practise this. There is no other way to learn.

The next time you're cooking a pot of tomato sauce, grab a spoon and a plate and practise saucing. Notice how the liquid spreads differently when poured directly, versus when it's zipped across the surface of the plate, and how it acts differently depending on if it's thick or thin. Notice how it splatters when poured from high. Take that into consideration when you're ladling soup. Do not ladle from an arm's reach away like some cocktail cowboy bartender. Bring the ladle to the bowl and tip it gently.

Balance

Good food has some balance of flavour and texture. This gives our palates the variety we crave, and the contrast highlights the dish's qualities (e.g., smoothness and crunchiness are more pronounced when paired together). This is why soup is simultaneously comforting and boring. Meals should not be monotonous. Consider the four food groups, and that vegetables are usually under-represented.

Good-looking food has some balance of shape and colour. I once worked for a chef whose solution to this was to sprinkle a handful of beets, ground in a food processer. It looked like Doc Holliday had coughed on the plate. Please don't add anything only for the sake of appearance. Everything should be there because it tastes good.

We love crunchiness. If you use it as an adjective on any restaurant menu, that will likely be the top-selling item. But if you used it for every dish, it would lose its power. Crunchiness is usually achieved through deep-frying, which is not so hard to do at home in a pot, but during dinner it becomes a hassle to deep-fry safely. Some thin items — such as basil, garlic, or chicken skin — can be deep-fried a few hours ahead of time and they will have a big impact as a garnish. Crunchiness could also be something as simple as adding crushed cashews to a bean salad.

Fresh herbs are a great way to add a light accent to heavy food. A link of braised beef short rib suddenly becomes a dish when it's topped with a few deep-fried garlic chips, some thyme leaves, and a spoonful of the reduced braising liquid.

A taco jammed with carnitas is delicious, but it comes alive when you add pickled onions and sour cream.

For colour, adding a little green or orange is something you might consider in the menu stage, choosing a different-coloured root vegetable, bean, or herb. What you want to avoid is a monochromatic plate, such as the whiteness of steamed grouper with rice and parsnips. Coloured oils — chili oil or pesto — have their place. Just keep them to a minimum, and don't use them to do the zigzag across the plate.

Remember that oils, even if they've been emulsified with parsley, will bleed. As they sit on the plate, the solids and liquids begin to separate, so they should be the last thing that goes on the plate.

THE SERVICE

 If you've made something special to accommodate a guest's dietary restrictions, serve that guest first. He or she will have a moment to feel special, rather than waiting at the back of the gluten bus.

Forget the formality of serving from the left. When placing food on the table, just aim to serve around guests. If two people are talking, don't lean in between them. Better to reach around them. Serve on the other side, unless, as previously suggested, you want to cut off their conversation so you can introduce your dish.

Whether the food is plated or family style, unless all dishes are on the table at once, you are serving a coursed meal, so there should probably be new plates and cutlery for each round.

When guests are eating tuna tartare with roasted beets, taking a pause, then eating rapini with pecorino Crotanese (don't tell me this sounds too fancy unless you have never put cheddar on top of broccoli), they should have fresh utensils. I'm not saying that people will be offended if you don't replace the cutlery for each course. In fact, some people will think, or even say, that it's not necessary, or that it's too chi-chi. But the bottom line is that no one wants to eat cheese off of a fork that smells like fish.

Do not rush the courses. Allow people time to breathe. Wait until everyone is done to clear plates, and even then give it a minute — don't spring into action the second the last guest puts down his or her fork. And do not clear plates until everyone has finished. In restaurants, this rule drives servers and cooks crazy. The kitchen is waiting for the signal to fire (start cooking) the next course. If they start too soon, the third course could be ready while the second course is still on the table.

But if all plates but one are cleared, that one person now feels rushed. While this internal logic may seem like common sense to the guest, I've seen a large table's tasting menu held up as one woman takes ten minutes to finally consume her last two spoonfuls of soup. This is where that server phrase "You still working on that?" comes from. They don't want to be pushy. They just need to know if you're done or not. Observation and body language usually communicate this. Guests will push a plate away, fold their arms, or balance fork and knife at the five o'clock position of their plate. But sometimes a guest likes to hold a fork indefinitely, like a drumstick or cigarette, sending mixed signals. Sometimes one has to ask.

I do the same thing in my home. Regular guests Lily and Zach eat at radically different paces. Zach can clean his plate and wipe it of sauce while Lily is still working her way through a spear of asparagus as if it were a T-bone. Over time, I've discovered a sort of marital osmosis, in which couples either needle each other about eating faster or slower, or actually eat off each other's plates, equalizing their rate of consumption.

If you are waiting for someone to finish, you can get started on some elements of the next course in the kitchen, such as slowly warming things up, counting out plates, or picking some fresh herbs. You can also wipe down the table. This is another restaurant trick that is pragmatically honest (if the table is dirty) but it also sends a non-confrontational message to that last, slowpoke eater.

Either way, this isn't a restaurant. The nice thing about being a friend instead of a servant is that we can say, "Either finish your story about your neighbour's poorly paved driveway or finish your last bite of asparagus, but stop trying to do both."

Once the lingerer has eaten the last mouthful, get those plates off the table. It is not such a huge amount of work to wash cutlery in between courses as well. Unless you have an industrial restaurant dishwasher in your home, which wishes a cycle in about two minutes, this means (gasp) washing by hand.

Now is the time to cash that investment you made earlier. Let your Helping Hands do rounds of dishes. Ask only those who have already volunteered, but expect others to volunteer as well, particularly if you make a big show of thanking the first person who helped out. Often, at the end of a great meal, those who didn't help out will squabble over the right to wash dishes, not wanting to be remembered as the only person who didn't pitch in.

None of this is to say that guests should be expected to help out. There are guests who believe that it would be an effrontery to be asked to wash dishes, and they are within their rights. Just don't waste the resources of volunteer labour.

THE WATER

 From the moment they take a seat at the table, guests should never be without water. As we learned in junior high health class, alcohol is a diuretic, meaning that it causes our body to lose water. Later in life, we learned that it is not awesome to be out-of-control drunk. And it is even less awesome still to wake up with a hangover.

Keep your guests hydrated. Don't wait until people are drunk to offer them water. If you do, expect them to ask, "What? You think I'm drunk?"

It's nice to constantly keep guests' glasses filled with water, but it's also a lot of unnecessary work. In the last five years, most mid-range restaurants have adapted. It used to be that a server would spend a great deal of the evening filling water glasses. Around the time that it became very unfashionable to sell bottled water, restaurants started leaving bottles and jugs on the table, filled from the tap, filtered or not.

This is an easy and elegant step to take at home, and you

don't need to buy one more kitchen thing. The next time you finish a liquor bottle, if you like the shape, just clean off the labels and use it for water. Whisky bottles are usually clear and tend to have wider bases than wine bottles (and in my home are finished quite often), so they're less likely to be knocked over. Lighter fluid will help remove any label adhesive. Keep two or three full bottles on hand so you can maintain a bottle on the table at all times. That way guests can help themselves.

If you walk around the table filling water, you'll seem like a butler. Instead, every time you reach to fill your own glass, first fill those around you. When they're full, pass the bottle down the table as a cue for others to help themselves. When it's empty, bring a full one. This way, you'll need to look after water (filling the bottles) only about once every hour.

THE DRINKING

As discussed in Chapter Two, if you are a wine person, then you know which wines to serve and when. If one of your friends is a wine person, allow him or her to take over this role. Trust me, your friend will accept the invitation. I never met a wine person who didn't want to drink, pour, and talk about wine, but such a person is not always available.

Your guests have brought you wine. Also, you have wine because, as stated, you are a grown-up. Which wine do you serve and which do you serve first? Know that you are under no moral obligation to serve the wine that your friends brought any more than if they brought you a book, you would have to read it right away. Over the course of the evening you will drink many bottles, so you'll probably get to it.

A guest might make a passive-aggressive stink about you not serving his or her wine. "Was there something wrong with the Chardonnay we brought?" They are basically like the aunt who expects you to wear the ugly Christmas sweater she knitted. Open their wine and pour them a glass. Just don't feel you have to drink it.

At some point in the evening you may have multiple bottles open. If you're refilling a glass that isn't empty, ask to make sure that you're pouring the right one. "Are you drinking the Malbec or are you still on the Cab?" It's pretty embarrassing to dump two wines together, but if you do, immediately take the glass away, rinse it, and pour a fresh one (unless the first wine was "pruno," prison toilet wine, in which case you have improved its overall composition).

Sometimes I rinse glasses in between wines, but not always. I find that most sommeliers expect that only when they're at a professional tasting, and the rest of the time they're happy to relax about a few drops at the bottom of the glass. The exception would be in switching from red to white, in which case I'll give it a rinse.

When you're pouring, don't fill the glasses more than a third. The wine needs oxygen to breathe. Hold the bottle by the base, not the neck. Finish the pour with a small twist, as you would with a spoonful of honey, to minimize the drip.

THE CONFRONTATION

I once had a hairdresser (I once had hair) who told me that she wouldn't let clients talk about politics or religion. Well, at a dinner party, people should talk about politics and religion. They should kibbitz and raise their voices and use the parts of their brains not activated by awards shows and conference calls. We should challenge each other and not be afraid to disagree. No topic should be forbidden among adults, but steer clear of death and disease. Let's not bring the room down.

Conversations can get out of hand. Always have a few questions up your sleeve that you can toss out at a moment's notice to divert the table's dialogue from the danger zone. "Any plans for the summer?" or "How did you spend your summer?" are the quintessential talk-show host diversionary questions. If they're good enough for David Letterman, they're good enough for us. I defy any group tension to withstand the question, "Did you know the mouth of a jellyfish is also its anus?"

Once guests behave badly, there is no easy way to deal with it. Part of inviting the right guests is avoiding those people who are prone to horrid behaviour. Unfortunately, some of our most entertaining friends are also the ones most likely to say something truly offensive.

Grown-ups, intelligent ones, can have intelligent disagreements. There's a satisfying crackle that goes through the room when one guest tells another, "I think you're full of crap and I'm going to tell you why." A good argument among respectfully disagreeing adults can make for a memorable evening.

I've already stated that a host and, by extension, a guest must endure certain indignities in aid of the group's enjoyment. That doesn't mean that we're all punching bags, hostages to the whim of a boorish person.

It can be grating to hear a guest go on about how much his or her house costs, the important people they know, all the great meals the guest has eaten elsewhere that were better than this one. However, it is not usually worth having a fight over.

But things get ugly when someone is being a bigot. In matters of social justice, it's go time. This isn't to say that we must get up on our hind legs at the first mention of something that *may* be sexist, racist, or homophobic. Having chosen to spend the evening in the company of these people, let us give them the benefit of the doubt that they are not all closet racists. But when we reach our threshold — the first, second, or third confirmed strike — it's time to call these people out.

The host or any guest can do this. If it's you, remember to focus on what they said, not who they are. Instead of, "Wow, you are a racist," tell them, "Wow, what you just said was racist."

There's no way it's going to end well, but you can at least dissect their words and explain what they mean to you, rather than attack the person and force him or her to behave defensively.

Try offering them a way out, an opportunity to recant or apologize, rather than demand it of them. Some people will fight just for the sake of it, or because they feel surrounded, so leave them an opening to escape. You'd like to get the evening back on track rather than derail it permanently, unless being right is more important to you.

And righteous though you may be, do not expect your guests to have your back. It's not that they disagree, but most people, whether from cowardice or some vestige of Victorian civility, will withdraw from a dinner fight like a vampire from the sun.

I was at a dinner where the host referred to her husband's music as gay. One guest decided that this made the host the perfect straw man to vent all his hostility toward homophobic language. As the two of them dug into their positions, the rest of the guests inched farther and farther to the other end of the table, in an effort at isolation.

If you, as a guest, become locked in an intractable argument, just leave. It's an unpleasant conclusion to your part of the night. But it might help the host and the other guests if one party takes themselves out of the equation, regardless of who's at fault.

If the evening does take an unpleasant turn, there is usually a collective will to fix things. During one dinner, forever referred to as "The Incident," a guest suddenly demanded to know why I hated her. When I didn't answer the question, it was repeated. If I had been at someone else's house, I would have just left. Bizarre and unexpected though it was, we had all been having such a nice time. And through sheer force of communal will, we managed to get the dinner back into its groove. Thinking back, I can hardly believe we were able to bring the evening back from such a dark extreme. Perhaps, for many people, this is what family dinners are like.

At a certain point it is worth considering that the night may be irreparably ruined. A guest can always leave, but a host cannot. So guests, if you think things have passed this threshold, consider an evacuation.

THE DRUNK

It's up to you whether you want your guests sober, tipsy, rosy-cheeked, raucous, or undergrad, but know your limits and try to keep everyone at the same pace. Prevent any one guest from getting significantly, embarrassingly, drunker than the rest. This is easier said than done. In fact, it was really easy for me to write that.

It's usually between drinks two and three that the heavy drinker shows you how fast they can drink. If you want everyone drunk, make sure you keep filling everyone else's glasses at the same rate. If you don't, slow things down. Do not leave the bottle on the table and certainly not within that one drunkard's reach.

However, the sort of person who is determined to get drunk will, which can make things uncomfortable for your other guests. This puts you in an awkward position. You don't want to make an issue of your guest's drunkenness at the table, though, along with bigotry, drunkenness may require a confrontation because that will just make people feel worse.

There are two courses to take:

1. Sweat it out. If you can tolerate their loutish behaviour for the rest of the evening, then don't bring attention to it. The next day, you can talk to them privately. Communicate clearly that their level of drunkenness was unacceptable. If you don't feel that this directness will be of any use, just blacklist them.

2. If their drunkenness is too out of control to tolerate,
    then take them aside (into the kitchen or a bedroom)
    and tell them, "You are too drunk and it's time for
    you to go to bed. I've called you a cab. Here's your
    coat. Please tell everyone you're not feeling well
    on your way out." Everyone else will understand.
    For the record, I have never had to do this, perhaps
    because my friends know that I do not tolerate sloppy,
    drunken tomfoolery.

This is also a time to ask your friends if they're driving,
or remind them. If your message from the invitation (see
Chapter One) has not been heeded, then pour accordingly. If
you know that guests are driving, limit their consumption of
wine while increasing their consumption of food and water.

If a guest has driven to your home and you see them
getting drunk, mention that. Ask them simply to choose
between not having another drink and parking the car
overnight. They can take a cab home. I've seen this done
very elegantly and effectively. A guest has a second drink
and says, "Y'know what? My car's on the street. I'm gonna
move it to the lot behind your house and leave it there."

This depends on the availability of parking, but you can
figure it out. There's really no excuse for drunk driving.

THREE PORK SHOULDER DISHES

New York City's Momofuku made a lot of friends with their bo ssäm, a massive slab of roasted pork shoulder accompanied by sauces and lettuce leaves for wrapping. As a result of its inclusion in their influential cookbook, it has become a birthday party staple among my friends, and I'm always happy to see it.

It's great to see friends learning to properly slow roast a big cut of meat but it's a shame to stop there as so much more that can be done with it. Pork shoulder is one of the best buys at the butcher shop, a powerful convergence of great flavour and value for price. The traditional bo ssäm method is simple and effective. If you can do that, consider some other uses for the pork. I suggest forgetting about wrapping the soft meat in bibb lettuce — not because the lettuce has the absorption of paper towel and inevitably leads to spilled sauces, but because it is expensive. If you need one head of lettuce for every three guests, it quickly becomes the most costly part of the meal.

It's a good lesson for slow cooking, showing how such a great texture and flavour can be achieved through time and patience rather than complicated techniques. Here are three other directions you can take it: tacos, rice bowl, and ragù for polenta. It's a good way to build on the skills you just learned, or to use up leftovers.

Pork Shoulder

4 lbs.	pork shoulder	2 kg
1/4 cup	sugar	60 mL
1/4 cup	kosher salt	60 mL
2 tbsp.	maple syrup	30 mL

Rub the pork with the sugar and salt. Refrigerate it in a sealed container overnight. Preheat the oven to 300°F (150°C). Mount the pork on a roasting rack and slide it into the oven. After a couple of hours the pork fat will start rendering. Use it to baste the meat. After four hours it will be soft, but after six hours it will be gooey. Finish the meat by rubbing it with maple syrup and cranking the oven to 500°F (260°C). Ten minutes should give the meat a good crust. Reserve extra rendered fat for future frying.

Serves four.

Tacos

It's pretty easy to turn the pork into taco meat. All you need are a few garnishes to really set it off. Use the pickle method from the rice bowl (see below) for red onions. Get fatty Mexican sour cream wherever you buy fresh tortillas. If you have some tarragon mayo left over from the tomato sandwiches, throw that in too. And here is a recipe for green salsa.

For the salsa

5	tomatillos, peeled, cored, and quartered	5
1/8	Spanish onion, peeled and roughly chopped	1/8
1	jalapeno, seeded and roughly chopped	1
1/4 bunch	cilantro, rinsed, dried, and roughly chopped	1/4 bunch
	salt to taste	

Blanch and shock the tomatillos by dropping them into boiling water for two minutes and then transferring them to a bowl of ice water. When they're cool, strain them and allow them to dry as much as possible. In a blender, purée them with onion, jalapeno, and cilantro. Season to taste.

For the tacos

1 lb.	6 in. (15 cm) tortillas	.45 kg
2 tsp.	cumin	10 mL
2 tsp.	coriander	10 mL
2 tsp.	black pepper	10 mL
½	Spanish onion, peeled and julienned	½
1 tbsp.	olive oil (or pork fat)	15 mL
1 tbsp.	chili powder (I use individually ground ancho and guajillo, but any mix should do)	15 mL
4 lbs.	pork shoulder, cooked and shredded (see above)	2 kg
	cilantro, chopped	

Preheat the oven to 250°F (120°C). Place the tortillas in an ovenproof pan. Cover with a damp towel. Keep in the oven until needed.

In a pan on high heat, toast the cumin and coriander seeds until smoking, about two minutes. Cool, then grind in a spice grinder with the black pepper.

In a large pan, sauté the onion in the olive oil or pork fat on medium heat until soft, about five minutes. Add the spices. Continue cooking for a minute, then fold in the shredded pork shoulder. Stir until warm.

To assemble: I like to put tacos together — pork, sour cream, pickled onion, cilantro, salsa — for guests because I find that if tacos are served family style, guests tend to overload each tortilla. If you want guests to help themselves, put everything in bowls and leave the tortillas in the pan, covered, so they'll retain some heat while on the table.

Serves four.

Rice Bowl

I like to eat anything on top of a bowl of rice (basmati is good, but I prefer the sticky Japanese rice), with pickled vegetables. Here are the basics.

For the rice

4 cups	koshihikari rice	1 L
6 cups	water	1.5 L
3/4 tsp.	kosher salt	3.75 mL
3/4 tsp.	sugar	3.75 mL
2 tsp.	rice vinegar	10 mL

Rinse the rice twice. Cover with water. Add the salt, sugar, and rice vinegar. Cook on low until firm but sticky, about fifteen minutes.

For the pickles

1	carrot	1
1	daikon	1
2 cups	water	500 mL
1/2 cup	rice vinegar	125 mL
2 tbsp.	salt	30 ml
2 tbsp.	sugar	30 mL

Peel and julienne the carrot and daikon. In a pot, boil the remaining ingredients until the salt and sugar are dissolved. Pack the vegetables in containers and cover with the brine. When cooled, cover and store in the fridge for months.

To assemble: Reheat the chopped pork in a pan with a bit of the reserved fat. Line four bowls with rice, pickled vegetables, and chopped pork. My fridge always has a half-dozen pickled things of my own making or store-bought. I will make this with any and every pickled item I can find, including kosher dill pickles, kimchee, sauerkraut, umeboshi, radishes, sunchokes, ginger, turnips left over from a Middle Eastern meal, chilies, giardiniera, and tsukemono. You can give it a bit more balance in texture and colour with a garnish of nori and cilantro.

Serves four.

Polenta and Ragù

Rather than slowly cooking meat in a tomato sauce, you've already got the meat, so it's just a matter of whipping up a fresh sauce. If you're making the pork expressly for this purpose, it's better to leave out that final hit of sugar when roasting.

For the ragù

1 tbsp.	olive oil	15 mL
2	garlic cloves, finely chopped	2
1/2	onion, finely chopped	1/2
1 cup	red wine	250 mL
6	tomatoes, finely chopped	6
4 lbs.	pork shoulder, cooked and shredded (see above)	2 kg
	salt	
	fresh basil	

In a large pot on medium heat, use the olive oil to sauté the garlic and onion until soft, about five minutes. Add the red wine and reduce until mostly evaporated. Add the tomatoes and pork. You can cook this down, but if the tomatoes are good, I prefer to keep it chunky.

For the polenta

6 cups	milk (or stock, or water)	1.5 L
1 1/2 cups	instant polenta	375 mL
1 tbsp.	butter (or pork fat)	15 mL
1 cup	grated Parmesan	250 mL
	salt	

In a large pot on medium heat, bring the liquid to a low boil (I like to use milk, but any liquid will do and I'll happily make a vegan version with water or mushroom stock and with engevita yeast in place of cheese). Add the polenta and whisk vigorously. Switch to a flexible spatula so you can scrape the corners of the pot. Stir in butter and cheese and season to taste. Serve immediately. If you want to make this in advance, bring it back to heat gently, but know that it'll need more liquid than you'd expect to rehydrate.

To assemble: Portion polenta into four bowls. Top with ragù and basil leaves.

Serves four.

CHAPTER EIGHT

YOU KNOW WHO'S PERFECT ALL THE TIME? Superman. And even he's spent the last seventy-five years getting his ass handed to him by Lex Luthor. The lesson here (aside from red kryptonite with meat, green kryptonite with fish) is that we should forgive ourselves our imperfections. Most of us repress our fears that we are terrible sons or daughters, mothers or fathers, or that, professionally, we suffer to some degree from the common imposter complex. Yet we'll trot out our feelings of failure over a roast beef for all to comment on. I'm calling BS on that. Unless you're prepared for a full-on *My Dinner with Andre*–style examination of your life choices and motivations, put a cork in your inner monologue. At the very least, a dinner party should not be a buffet of insecurities. The first step toward having a little confidence in your cooking is letting go of the fantasy of perfection.

THE FEEDBACK AND THE PERFECTION

Do not introduce food by telling your guests that it's no good. As crazy as that sounds, it happens all the time.

"Oh, this didn't turn out the way I'd hoped," says the host, handing us his or her insecurity on a plate. "It's not very good, but the directions were confusing," the host adds. "And I couldn't find all the ingredients." It's like offering to help someone with their taxes and then telling them that you're terrible with numbers.

If you think what you've cooked is bad, you shouldn't be serving it. Food does not need to be perfect. Maybe it does in a restaurant, where you would be shocked if your server brought the food you'd ordered and told you it was no good. Home cooking does not need to be stellar. It needs to be good, hot, on time, and plentiful.

If what you've cooked is truly disastrous — burnt to a crisp, dried out, inedibly salty, or spoiled — then do not serve it. Pick up a phone and order a pizza, and do it without consulting your guests, because if you tell them that you've burned the roast, they'll insist that it's fine, that there's no need to order out when you've worked so hard cooking. But they'll be liars, and you'll see it on their faces when they take a bite.

Just call in the cavalry and play it off for laughs. "Guys, I hope you like pizza," you tell them, "because a government inspector would not let me serve this roast, even to a dog." Tell them you called the order in fifteen minutes ago so there's no turning back.

If you want an honest evaluation of how you did, go ahead and ask, but wait until the day after. Do not solicit critical feedback at the table. Do not ask your friends how the food is. Do not say, "No, really, tell me."

Because you already know. If people make grunting and ooh-ing sounds, they like it. If they avoid saying anything about it, it's passable. If they say it's "interesting" or "unique," they don't like it. Absorb this and learn from it. Don't pout. Sometimes people are so caught up in conversation that the food becomes background. This might hurt our feelings as cooks, but it's a mark of success as hosts. Smile.

This isn't a community college theatre class, where we go around the circle criticizing each other's technique. That puts people on the spot. And in the end, all any host wants to hear is that everything was great. In the absence of that validation, suck it up.

If you have a friend whose opinion you really respect, ask him or her later, not in front of everyone. Send your friend an email. After the fact, honesty becomes a virtue again. While we're on stage, we don't pick the show apart.

Though if you are my friend Jesse Brown, you already know how your cooking was: too clovey.

ON INSISTENCE

Guests, you may wind up at the table of a host who demands that you criticize their food. They have watched too much make-believe cooking on television and they think that this drama is part of the evening. Hold your ground, as you would with a bear. Do not show signs of fear and do not try to run away from the conversation. Lie. Plenty of times I could've said, and meant, "The food was okay, but the company was fantastic." But no one wants to hear that. They only want compliments. If they demand to know what you thought of a dish, it was great. If they get specific, asking about the leeks, then the leeks were the best part. If they want more, they can subpoena you. And talk to your lawyer.

The whole point of the evening is to enjoy each other's company with the aid of good food and wine. But if we're being honest, then sure, there's a subtext of competition. All that stuff that I said doesn't

matter — the size of your home, the elegance of your stemware, the deliciousness of your food — does, in fact, matter, but it matters only to our egos, to the part of us that every bit of common sense and every spiritual belief system (expect maybe Objectivism) teaches us to rise above.

Though we try not to, we are keeping a running tab of how much everyone else earns, how well-behaved their children are, or how amusingly they tell a story. When we have people over to our homes, it can feel like show-and-tell day at the shrink's office, time to feel good or bad about ourselves, our belongings, our charisma, our choices. The food we've cooked is a physical manifestation of all that.

But it's not about us. Save that analysis for after the party, when you and your husband or wife are cleaning up. Your friends, on their way home, will be doing the same thing, analyzing what went right and what went wrong, while you, at home, are dissecting who was a good guest and who was a bad guest. For that moment, save your thoughts about how dry the potatoes were.

I have not always heeded my own advice, or perhaps I've just had to learn the hard way that no one really wants your opinion on his or her cooking. Though I used to get paid to write restaurant reviews, from time to time I've dished it out for free, with disastrous results. I offer these stories as a warning to travellers who may be foolish enough to tread this path with their friends.

One time I went to a new restaurant with a pal. We sat at the bar. I was friends with one of the servers and during each course, she came to ask what I thought. The bartender and one of the owners also made inquiries with each dish. I smiled and nodded. Truthfully, it was all quite good. During one dish I responded to the bartender that it needed salt. Soon the chef came to the table to ask me why I didn't like the dish and then told me why I was wrong. "It's a handmade tofu," he explained, "and the subtlety would be ruined if seasoned like the rest of the dishes." He walked away without saying goodbye. A week later a friend ate there and the staff asked her, "What's with your asshole friend Corey?"

One time my friend Jesse was serving chile en nogada, a Mexican dish that he was excited about. He asked me how it tasted. I told him it was good, which it was. Again and again he asked, insisting that there must be something, some small area for improvement. I told him that it was a little clovey. "A little clovey?" he repeated, gazing back at me as if I'd desecrated his family's tomb. In the years since, at every meal with Jesse, he has never failed to inquire if my food is too clovey.

Eventually it became a running gag. But at first it was a clear indication that, though he asked for feedback, he didn't want to hear anything more than those other chefs did. "It's delicious, chef," is what we should say. "Your best work yet."

THE PORTIONING

If you reach a moment in your dinner party (or in your life, really) when your primary fear is that your guests may be too full, this is one of those good problems, like people who worry that they enjoy jogging too much. Congratulations, you've won life.

As we discussed in the menu planning stages, it is difficult to know how much to make. Don't feel bad. The other day at the grocer's I couldn't help but overhear with two guys debating how many potatoes they needed for dinner. They were both professional cooks, planning a dinner party for a friend. They were comfortable with buying whole fish and butchering it for ceviche, or improvising dishes based on what they found at the market. One of them insisted on having one pound of potatoes per guest, which is a monstrous amount. Just know that even professionals have trouble guessing how much people will eat.

It is easy to know when people are full. They will emit sounds, possibly belch depending on your or their culture's acceptance of that sort of thing, and say things like, "Whoa, there is more?" Watch and listen for these unsubtle signs. Do not force your guests to eat too much out of politeness.

It will happen in different stages with different guests because — and I'm going to state the obvious here — big people tend to eat more than little people. This isn't always true, but you can usually bank on it. I have a couple of friends who are six feet five inches tall and I try to serve them the one piece of beef that's bigger than the others or the extra potato. They're the ones who finish first and look over their shoulders to see if there's more. These people are the reason that you always make a little extra. When you see they've still got that hungry look on their face or (and I swear to you this happens all the time) are greedily eyeing their wife's plate, surprise them with, "There's more stuffing in the pan." You will see them light up. Every guest deserves satisfaction.

In the menu planning stage, we introduced the idea of preparing a last course with a negotiable amount. Now it may be time to put this into effect. You've watched for the signs, seen guests leaning back, slapping their bellies, pushing their plates away. If you've got more food coming, you may need to call an audible. If I understand my football reference correctly (and I probably don't), this is when the quarterback serves the wide receiver only half as much mashed potatoes as originally planned. Or is that lacrosse?

When they see you plating the last course, they'll make more groaning sounds. Translation: "Dear host, please don't be offended if we don't finish this food. It's not that we don't like it, but we are very full." But once they've seen the small amount you've plated, they will relax and discover that they do indeed have a little more space in their bellies. And of course, everyone miraculously has more room for desert.

Portioning is also what they call "a teachable moment," albeit a small one. As you see guests getting full, take a moment to think of how much they've eaten. This will help you in future dinner parties. Once you've seen that threshold a number of times, you'll grow comfortable in planning portions. Again, as Miyamoto says, "You must practise this. There is no other way."

Let the unserved food cool before placing it in the fridge, but get it in there while it's still on your mind. You don't want to discover, after spending the rest of the evening eating dessert and drinking, that you've left the meat out for hours.

THE DESSERT

We worry over dessert, yet rarely need to. In all likelihood, people are pretty full at the end of dinner. They should be. What most of us want is a bite or two of something chocolatey, so my first word on dessert is to caution against overdoing it. It's heartbreaking to see a beautiful pie come out of the oven, the meringue top tinged with a little brown, when no one has any desire to eat it. I have a friend who loves to bake, but he also loves to cook rich, fatty food and insists on ladling out seconds. By dinner's end, he's stuffed us with brisket and bread, yet he'll also make not just pie, but cake and cookies as well.

No one ever complains that there's too much dessert, but we often feel bad if we don't eat it. Sometimes, when full to bursting, we feel worse if we do. Filter this through the perspective of age as well. When I was twenty-five, I slept next to a drawer full of candy, which I would actually snack on during the night. But most of us, as we age, first start gaining weight, then start worrying, at the behest of doctors and spouses, about our hearts and all that stuff.

Because I host a dinner every week, and because I'm now older and metabolize sugar more slowly than I once did, I wish we could do away with dessert. However, whenever I think that, I remember that my guests do not attend a dinner party every week and that, as a guest in someone's house, dessert is expected. They have worked hard all week and have earned their slice of pie.

Not only should you not serve too much dessert, you should not serve it too quickly. Allow guests time to digest their meal. Even if you've taken a more relaxed approach to the courses (reusing cutlery and plates), treat dessert as a separate act. Completely clear and wipe down the table. Expect people to help out at this point, if for no other reason than that they need to stand and stretch.

If you are offering tea or coffee, ask guests before you serve dessert. Some people need to have their coffee and cake at the same time and can become oddly unhinged if they are served a slice of cake and told that they'll have to wait while coffee is brewing.

I don't bake much. The whole process feels entirely different to me from cooking, but on occasion I'll try out a recipe, during which time all electronic devices in the home must be turned off so I can completely focus on the printed word. Instead, I prefer to assign dessert to one of my guests. When I have a friend who likes to bake, then it's an easy fit. This takes a load off the host and also provides an easy answer to "What can I bring?"

ON COFFEE

When I was a kid it was unthinkable to have a holiday dinner without coffee. My family didn't drink much wine, but they stayed up late doing caffeine. At my grandmother's for Rosh Hashanah, my aunt's house for Passover, or our apartment for Hannukah (where my father didn't even drink coffee), the meals were followed by a solicitation for drink orders, resulting in two batches of coffee — regular and decaf — being brewed, plus a pot of tea. No one drinks coffee after dinner anymore.

Just before serving dessert, I'll often ask if anyone would like a cup. Except for a few who have requested decaf (which is to coffee what white chocolate is to chocolate), I've had exactly two people say yes.

Often coffee drinking is not about the gastronomic experience. The markers we use to discuss and grade coffee — aroma, balance, acidity, sweetness, finish — are a smokescreen for the normalized abuse of stimulants. It's about getting high. And getting high is usually about avoiding reality. Talk to any recovering addict and they'll tell you that their use was about escaping bad times and prolonging good times. In the morning, we drink coffee to change our perception of an unpleasant reality — that

we are tired but we must work. After dinner, if we drink coffee it is because we're enjoying the company of friends, so we look for an excuse to extend that experience.

There is a sublime sense of closure to coffee at the end of a huge meal, when most of us are sleepy and a little espresso isn't going to keep us up (though it will likely result in a less restful sleep). I usually find that at the end of a good dinner party, around 11 p.m., a group will stay talking for an extra hour, with nothing more to eat or drink. Culturally, in North America, coffee is no longer an expectation. I don't know anyone who will drink decaffeinated coffee, but if you do, it's little trouble to keep a small batch in the freezer.

"A modern meal," writes Adam Gopnik, "is a drama unfolding between the Opening Drink and the Concluding Coffee, with the several acts passing between the libations." In his essay "Who Made the Restaurant?" he adds, "French cooking was made not merely in the space between caffeine and alcohol but in the simultaneous presence of both, thus blending, in sequence, the two drugs by which modern people shape their lives. Good food takes place in the head space between them."

I have had Adam Gopnik over for dinner, and even he passed on the coffee.

If dessert is store-bought, guests will have less trouble saying no. If, however, it's homemade, they will have a slice, just to be polite. When they say, "just a sliver," be respectful of that. If a guest has brought dessert, particularly if he or she made it, serve it with the same respect and care that you did your own dishes. Do not slap it on the table as an afterthought. One last tip: When slicing cake, run the knife under hot water in between each slice. You'll get a clean cut every time and avoid the messy buildup on the side.

REESE'S RICE PUDDING

This is a mashup (that means I stole two ideas to create one I can call my own without being sued) of Jennifer McLagan's recipe for bone marrow rice pudding from her book *Fat* and a basic risotto.

I think that it's a hit because it removes the one variable of rice pudding that is commonly unpopular: the raisins. And it replaces the offending dried fruit with the flavour of Reese's peanut butter and chocolate, which is hardly peanut butter or chocolate but is nonetheless insanely delicious.

7 cups	milk	1.75 L
1	vanilla bean	1
1 1/3 cups	Arborio rice	330 mL
pinch	salt	pinch
1/2 cup	sugar	125 mL
3	eggs	3
1 1/2 tbsp.	bourbon or rum	7.5 mL
1	Reese's Peanut Butter Bar or 3 Peanut Butter Cups, chopped	1

In a saucepot, gently heat the milk and the vanilla bean, without boiling.

In a large pan, toast the rice for a few minutes on low heat. As you would for risotto, slowly ladle in the milk, stirring constantly, letting each batch evaporate before adding more. Incorporating all the milk, cook until the rice is tender but not soft, about eighteen minutes. In a mixing bowl, whisk the sugar, salt, eggs, liquor, and chocolate. Fold into the rice pudding, cook for a couple more minutes, and serve warm.

If preparing in advance, cook the rice halfway, for nine minutes. Transfer to a tray, spread flat, and allow to cool. When ready to serve it for dessert, slowly heat it back up to a light simmer. Fold in the sugar, eggs, liquor, and chocolate, stirring, until cooked through.

CHAPTER NINE

THOSE MILK PEOPLE HAD THE RIGHT IDEA. Everything should have an expiration date: jobs, marriages, interviews, biopics, dinner guests. I believe that when we keep doing something past its prime, the experience sours.

I understand the compulsion. When things are going well, when everyone is having fun, there is an unspoken communal will to continue. But that's just when you should be thinking of an exit strategy. When we are done with an evening, it can be excruciatingly uncomfortable that the other parties involved want to keep it going.

Take a page out of the comedian's handbook and always go out on a high note, because that's how they'll remember you. I'm not saying that if you get a big laugh at 8 p.m. you should say, "You've been a great audience, thanks for coming out," and walk off the stage, but it's better to leave them wanting more.

THE END

 It's hard to know when the night is over. In restaurant etiquette, a server never asks anyone to leave and never brings a bill without being asked (or at least they shouldn't, and it's considered rude), so they use cues. Asking, "Can I get you anything else?" means you should ask for the bill. Wiping tables and putting up chairs means the restaurant is closing.

One of the splendid advantages of dining at home is that there is no closing time. No one is waiting to take our table. The establishment is not losing money if we linger after our meal without spending more. However, the dinner party's timeline is not infinite, and we can use the professional server's techniques to draw the evening to a conclusion.

Yawning means you're tired. Tidying up around guests means you want them out. The problem is, your guests may be drunk and not pick up on social cues.

These, however, are our guests, not our clients. At home we are not bound by the propriety of servitude. If subtlety isn't working, just tell your guests to get out. You don't have to be a lout about it. Something softer such as "Well, I need to go to bed" or "I wish we could go all night, but I've got an early-morning squash game" should suffice. I don't know that squash is a real game — frankly, the sport sounds made up — but I have friends who claim this as a reason for early rising.

There are people (and this is where my understanding of human nature runs dry) who think there is some inherent rudeness in calling it a night, or think that it is a competition with the other guests in which whoever goes home first loses. This is rubbish. If anything, it's considerate to not overstay your welcome.

Most of the time, if you're looking, you'll see couples attempting to wordlessly communicate with each other, gauging their desire to leave. They'll glance at their watches and use their eyes to point toward the door. There's that hand on the shoulder that says, "Honey, I'm ready for bed" or "Honey, you're ready for bed." Whichever way the wind blows, the message is, "Honey, start paying attention to me, because one of us is ready to go home."

If you're catching these signals, you can help these poor souls. Let them off the hook by pointing out, "Susie, I think Paloma is about to fall asleep. Maybe it's time to get her to bed."

You might also offer up leftovers. This is another case where economic and cultural background take precedence. Some think it gauche to take home a "doggie bag." Likely that term has not helped the concept's acceptance, but I think that many more people are anti-waste. Most people I know are quite busy and only too happy to accept a ready-made meal.

THE NIGHTCAP

 A nightcap can be a great or terrible way to end the evening. As my shelf of liquors has grown, I've gotten in the habit of offering guests a Scotch or bourbon. (Now I feel self-conscious that I don't have any good brandy.) This is usually toward the evening's close, as everything is winding down. If you are prepared for everyone to stay at least another hour, by all means place a bottle on the table. Just know that it will blur the concept of time.

Not everyone is in agreement that a nightcap is a drink just before leaving. The word alone is insufficient to communicate that message. If you are about ready for guests to leave, do not provide any additional drinks without strings attached.

If it's a drink for the road, make two things clear:

1. This last drink signals the end. Invoke your impending sleep and your guests' impending departure.

2. No one who is driving home should have a drink for the road. But on a cold winter's night, those who are walking or travelling by train, bus, or streetcar can do well with something to keep them warm and giggly on the journey home. This can be introduced and assessed with "Well, if you're walking home, how about one for the road?"

In addition to calling them a taxi, we could also invite them to sleep over. Hopefully, our friends can accept this without throwing a tantrum and forcing us to hide their car keys. If not, guess who's never invited again?

I frequently I have leftover dessert. The next morning, rather than eating half a pie for breakfast, I earmark it for my butcher. Since he and I are on a first-name basis, it is socially acceptable for me to show up with half a pie for him and his employees.

Some guests leave all at once, as if they just heard that the cops are coming and they have to scramble down the fire escape. Others will let one couple say their goodnights, then stay another ten minutes. I like this style. It's a more gradual wind-down. There's nothing you can do to enforce it. A good friend may offer to stay and help clean up. By all means, say yes.

If you've stored coats in a closet or your room, bring them to the departing guests. Some people will perceive a social barrier about entering your bedroom to fetch their coat. Holding a coat up so that its wearer can slip into it is an old-timey gesture that I adore. It seems like an affectation, but it is a tiny effort and always appreciated by a man or woman.

KISSES, HUGS, AND HANDSHAKES

There is a potential for awkwardness in our farewells. We don't want to leave a bad taste at the end of the night by shaking someone's hand when the person wants a hug or groping someone who was going for a high-five. Don't let me force you into a level of social intimacy that you're not comfortable with, but be prepared for hugs and kisses.

This all depends on who you are, who your guests are, and how well you know each other. Some people are on a hug-hello basis with everyone, while others are strictly handshakers.

The people in your life likely all have a designated physical greeting: a handshake for the boss; a kiss on the cheek for a friend's wife; a hug for a mom. However, at the end of an evening, if it's been wonderful, you may find that that relationship has changed.

Having strangers over every week, I usually find that by the end of the night we've upgraded from a handshake to a kiss on the cheek. The key to not fumbling this is to read their body language and leave yourself open. First, allow other people to take the initiative. If someone's wife, whom you've never met, had a great time and wants to give you a big hug, then you return that hug. But do not touch her hair, even if that is your particular fetish.

If you let guests get to the door ahead of you, they'll form a gridlock, as no one wants to step through the portal without their last goodbye. Try to position yourself by the door so that everyone has to proceed past you, the way that people will line up at a wedding to greet the bride and groom. To avoid the double-goodbye, do this as they're gathering their shoes. As they file past you into the night, each one will likely move in for some type of greeting. Use your complicated animal brain to read their movements and lean into it. As I cannot keep track of which friends require single, double, or (good lord) triple kisses on the cheek, I have simplified my life by only giving out one kiss per customer.

I think the Japanese have simplified everything with a bow. Then again, the exact degree of a Japanese bow denotes how much respect is being offered by the bower to the bowee, so maybe it's not so much simple as it is gender-neutral. Perhaps we could just be like the military and salute.

THE CLEANUP

Once the last guest has left, you're probably tired, and rightfully so. If you want to go ahead and jump into bed, leaving the dishes for the morning, no one's judging you — no one except me.

Just know, as your head hits the pillow, that somewhere out there, another dinner party host is doing a full cleanup. That host will wake up to a tidy home, get that promotion, and be 30 percent less likely to go bald, and his or her children will get into better schools. But if you're really tired, sure, leave the dishes for the morning.

If you're a couple, or if one friend has stayed behind, the cleanup is fun because you get to do the post-mortem. All those things that you kept your mouth shut about during the dinner can all come tumbling out. Did you notice that Lloyd demanded I open his terrible wine? Could you believe Mark's totally bogus last-minute allergy to Brussels sprouts? And what is going on with Colin's racist boyfriend Ian, Mr. "Hitler had some good ideas"?

Even if I'm by myself, I like using the time to recount what went wrong and what went right, who I need to thank, and who I need to apologize to. By the time the evening has been examined, the last of the dishes are washed and the table's been wiped down.

But I don't clean everything. After breaking a lot of wineglasses, I have learned to leave them for the morning. Good stemware needs a washing and then a wiping. Between the thinness of the glass and the thickness of adult hands, it's too much delicate work to be done after midnight. Just before you go to bed, do you want to be bandaging your hand or picking glass out of the sink's drain? Since a friend convinced me to leave wineglasses for the morning, I've stopped breaking them.

BEANS AND GRAINS

We should all learn to cook with beans and grains for three reasons:

1. Getting protein from non-animal sources is good for our bodies.

2. Learning to cook with beans and grains makes it easier to accommodate vegetarians.

3. Beans and grains are inexpensive.

Dried chickpeas cost about $2 a pound. Barley is half of that. A cup of barley costs me 44 cents. Cooked, it will expand to about 4 cups.

In order to take advantage of these ingredients, we must first learn the technique of cooking beans and grains. Then we must learn how to use them in a dish.

Grains such as barley and quinoa benefit from a light toasting. The only trick to cooking them is to keep the water at a low boil. If you cook barley at a rolling boil, it becomes gluey.

Dried beans need to be soaked for a couple of hours before cooking, though lentils, which are small and cook quickly, do not. Again, keep the water at a low boil when cooking, or the beans will be torn apart and mushy. Navy or black beans will take longer to cook than kidney beans or chickpeas, but in general expect about thirty to forty minutes. Once cooked, you can store them in the fridge for up to a week before using. Just remember to cool them properly by laying them out flat on a cookie sheet. If piled in a bowl, hot food will continue to steam.

The larger challenge is how to use these ingredients.

Beans and grains are very good sponges for flavour. They have lots of surface area to absorb sauces, but not so much character that they'll overwhelm other elements in the dish. Think of them as a coat of primer paint. They provide a platform for the main ingredient and make its job easier.

Here are a few things I like to do with barley, quinoa, and chickpeas. These elements aren't interchangeable (I'd pair dates with quinoa or barley, but not with chickpeas). Cooking them separately, then combining them with different vegetables or proteins or cheeses, should drive home how modular they are. After you make one or two of these dishes as a side, a salad, or a base for a simple roast chicken breast, you might start to consider all the flavours that can stick to the lowly bean.

Barley and Brussels Sprouts Salad

12	Brussels sprouts, tails removed and sliced in half	12
1 cup	toasted almonds	250 mL
2	apples, finely diced	2
1	lemon	1
6 cups	cooked barley (start with 2 cups/500 mL dry)	1.5 L
3	celery stalks, finely diced	3
1 bunch	celery leaves	1 bunch
	salt and pepper	

Blanch and shock the Brussels sprouts by dropping them in a pot of boiling water until soft, about three minutes, then transferring to ice water until cool. Strain and pat with paper towels to dry. Slice into strips.

Using a mortar and pestle, or a food processor on pulse, lightly crush the almonds so they are pebbles, but not quite dust.

Toss the diced apples with a squeeze of lemon juice to pre-vent them from oxidizing.

In a large mixing bowl, combine all ingredients. Season to taste with salt and pepper.

Serves four.

Taco Salad

8 cups	cooked chickpeas (2.5 cups/625 mL dried)	2 L
2	tomatoes, cored and diced	2
6	tomatillos, peeled, cored, and diced	6
1	Spanish onion, peeled and diced to the size of cooked chickpeas	1
1	lime, juice of	1
1	bird's eye chili, finely chopped	1
	salt	
1 lb.	tortilla chips (see Chapter Four)	.45 kg
1/4 cup	Mexican sour cream	60 mL
3	scallions, finely diced	3

In a large mixing bowl, combine the cooked chickpeas, toma-toes, tomatillos, and Spanish onion with lime juice and chili. Mix, seasoning to taste. Assemble in four bowls with tortilla chips. Drizzle with the sour cream. Sprinkle with the scallions.

Mexican sour cream is closer to crème fraîche. If you can't find it in a Latin grocery store, you could try some crumbly feta.

Serves four.

QUINOA AND DATE SALAD

6	Medjool dates	6
1/2 cup	roasted almonds	125 mL
1/2 cup	quinoa	125 mL
splash	olive oil	splash
1	lemon, zest of	1
1 tbsp.	grated ginger	15 mL
1/2 tsp.	cinnamon	2.5 mL
	salt and pepper to taste	
1/2 cup	soft goat cheese	125 mL

Pit and dice the dates.

In a food processor or with a mortar and pestle, loosely crush the almonds without turning them into paste.

Heat a large pot of water to a medium boil. Add the quinoa. Cook until soft but still crunchy, about twenty minutes. Strain. Mix with the olive oil, lemon zest, ginger, cinnamon, dates, and half of almonds. Season to taste with salt and pepper. Assemble in bowls. Garnish the with remaining almonds and the crumbled goat cheese, torn into chunks.

Serves four.

CHAPTER TEN

"**J**USTICE SHOULD NOT ONLY BE DONE," DECREED Lord Chief Justice Gordon Hewart, "but should manifestly and undoubtedly be seen to be done." Let this axiom wash over the thanking process.

There is a difference between appreciation and showing appreciation. And if we want it to count, to be clear, we must make a display of it, no matter how much it feels like your stepmother is forcing you to write thank-you notes to everyone who came to your bar mitzvah.

THE THANK YOU

 We used to believe that man was elevated above animal by our use of tools. Then Jane Goodall observed chimpanzees using sticks to pull delicious termites from their mounds, and we were cast back down among our savage ancestors.

Now we know that what truly separates us from the beasts of the jungle is a thank-you letter. I'd like to see some hyena send even so much as an appreciative text message, thanking a vulture for sharing a gazelle carcass.

I have received all manner of thank-you gestures. Guests have sent emails, cards, texts, and tweets. They've left Nutella in my mailbox and stopped by with heads of broccoli. They've even called, which I don't care for since, outside of hosting a dinner party every week, I'm actually a bit of a misanthrope and don't like talking on the phone.

What these all have in common is that they are gestures, symbolic acts undertaken to communicate one person's gratitude to another. No one owes us anything, but the act of taking time to express a nice sentiment is always worth it.

Guests, I know you said the words "thank you" at the end of the night. It may seem redundant to say it again, but we say thank you to a stranger for holding a door open for us. A friend who has hosted a dinner deserves a little more.

I used to be uptight about how I was thanked. Now I'll take whatever I can get. It's just the acknowledgement that's important. I wouldn't say that any thank you is superior to another, but I would imply it.

It's nice to get something thoughtfully written. We don't need to get too elaborate, going into a play-by-play synopsis of the evening. Two sentences are all anyone needs to get this message across. A handwritten card, or any mail that isn't a bill or a flyer, is so rare these days that it's a treat.

Couples, you can co-thank, but make it clear that it's from both of you by using the first-person plural. "I had a great time," is not from both of you. Maybe you've gotten used to living for two as a default lifestyle, but your language choices need to reflect that. It's "We had a great time. Thanks for dinner."

Guests, send a thank you within one week of the dinner. Hosts, don't hold it against people if you don't get a thank you. Remember that your friends are busy, and also consider their extenuating circumstances. Sometimes people are getting on a plane the next morning, so sending a thank-you email is not their first priority.

THE RECIPROCATION

Like it or not, reciprocation makes the world go around. I phrase it this way because there are some who bristle at the mention of tit-for-tat, quid pro quo, one hand washing the other, etc. Some might rightfully suggest that it is gauche to keep a ledger of our social credits and debits, and they're right. It is tacky. But it is also how life works.

When we find ourselves in relationships, social or

professional, where one party is doing all the giving and the other is doing all the taking, resentment will build up. Whether one person is buying all the milk, changing all the diapers, or choosing all the movies, it's got to be balanced by something, or eventually it's going to pop. We'll be flossing one night, a reasonable prevention against the buildup of plaque, and we'll ask our partner, "Honey, have you noticed that we've had over the Fidermens like, six times, and they've never invited us for dinner?"

The answer to this is silence. We don't like acknowledging a friendship imbalance, that we are doing more for someone than they do for us. It may seem mercenary to keep a social ledger, because that's not what friendship is. It's just better to stay one step ahead of this before it becomes a problem.

Hosting a good dinner should mean being invited to another, but not everyone wants to host. Don't be pissed if friends never invite you. Maybe they don't host dinner parties. Some people don't cook, don't have a suitable dinner table, or just don't like having guests in their home. They are entitled to that, but if these are friends you socialize with regularly, and you are inviting them over regularly, then they should reciprocate in some way. The most obvious way to do that is for them to pick up the bill the next time you're eating out together.

A lady or gentleman wouldn't dream of declaring this sort of social debt, but then a lady or gentleman also wouldn't express that, while they've enjoyed several great meals at your home and would love to have you over, they don't cook, or are nervous about cooking for you. Now I respect the duplicity of that statement. It's a brilliant bit of legalese that translates as "my inadequacy excuses me from the golden rule." That line is to the thank you what "I'm sorry you feel that way" is to the apology.

If you keep hearing this from friends, it is the signal to play your trump card. "Oh, you don't have to have us over," you say. "You can just buy dinner the next time we're out."

CORNBREAD

I have eaten a hundred different cornbreads. Some had pockets of corn or cheddar. Some were dense, others crumbly. I've had them baked as little cakes and sliced from big loaves. As long as it is good, there is no firm rule on how a cornbread should be. Here is a recipe that I got from Toronto chef Cory Vitiello. I've adjusted it slightly, just as he changed it from whoever taught him, and you will add or subtract based on what you like about it.

2 1/2 cups	all-purpose white flour	625 mL
1 1/4 cups	uncooked polenta	310 mL
1/4 cup	stone-ground cornmeal	60 mL
2 tbsp.	baking powder	30 mL
1 tsp.	sea salt	5 mL
1/3 cup	sugar	80 mL
1 cup	corn kernels	250 mL
1	jalapeno, finely chopped and sautéed	1
2	eggs	2
1/8 cup	unsalted butter, melted	30 mL
1 1/2 cups	buttermilk	375 mL
1 tbsp.	pork fat or butter	15 mL

Preheat the oven to 350°F (175°C).

Using your fingers, mix all dry ingredients together, including the corn kernels, and jalapeno. In a separate bowl, whisk the eggs. Whisk the butter and buttermilk into the eggs. Pour the wet ingredients into the dry and, switching to a spatula, mix together until all of the flour is incorporated.

Preheat a 12-in. (30.5 cm) cast-iron pan with pork fat or butter. Pour the batter into the pan.

Bake for about forty minutes or until a toothpick comes out fairly clean from the middle. Allow five minutes to cool before slicing.

Now that you've got the cornbread, what can you do with it?

I find that if cornbread is good and warm, and if there is plenty of butter on the table, it's all people want to eat. If you're serving it as a side with, say, a brined and roasted pork loin and red-eye gravy, warm it up before serving. I'd be glad to have it with a fried slice of the braised beef cheek from Chapter Three or the ceviche from Chapter One. Here are a couple of other ideas.

CORNBREAD PANZANELLA

	olive oil	
1	red onion	1
4	chorizo sausages	4
1	cornbread	1
4	tomatoes, sliced into bite-sized cubes	4
4	sprigs of oregano, leaves of	4

In a large pan with a splash of olive oil, cook the onion on low heat until caramelized, about fifteen minutes.

Preheat the oven to 400°F (204°C).

In a large cast-iron pan on high heat, sear sausages on all sides and slide the pan into the oven. Turning every few minutes, cook the sausages through, about ten minutes.

Cut the cornbread into large cubes, the same size as the tomatoes. Slice the cooked sausages into a similar size.

In a large mixing bowl, combine all ingredients. Add the cornbread cubes last so the tomatoes won't make them soggy.

Serves six.

CORNBREAD GRILLED CHEESE

How much direction do you need for this one?

Considering its richness, you might not want to serve sandwich-sized portions of this. Maybe whip up a batch and slice it into three-bite portions for an appetizer.

8	cornbread slices	8
8	aged Cheddar slices	8
4	cooked bacon strips	4
2 tbsp.	unsalted butter	30 mL

Slice the cornbread ½ in. (1.25 cm) thick. Assemble sandwiches with Cheddar and bacon on the inside.

On a low heat, melt butter in a cast-iron pan. Slowly brown the sandwiches on one side, about four minutes. Melt more butter in the pan and flip. Cook on the second side until the cheese melts.

Serves four.

AFTERWORD

WANT EVERYONE'S DINNER PARTY TO BE FUN. WITH a book of rules, plus the running score of thank you notes and reciprocations, it might seem to be more business than personal. And if that happens, it's time to take a step back.

Though gleaned from years of hosting on a regular basis, the instructions in this book are only guidelines. They are not the Ten Commandments or the sacred scrolls (sorry, but grade five Hebrew school and *Planet of the Apes* are all I know from religion).

The key word is flexible.

Yes, I send thank-you notes to my friends. And I try to do nice things in exchange for the nice things they do for me. But I don't sit at home with an abacus, calculating each friend's value, like some vengeful Santa Claus. It's all predicated on the idea that we like each other, that we want to spend time together. If Jesse forgets to send me a thank you for dinner, I'm not going to hold it against him. Aside from devoting pages and pages in this book to publicly shaming him, I probably wouldn't even mention it.

The other night I went over to Jesse's to store my patio cushions in his basement for the winter. "Bring me something," he requested. I brought leftovers from the dinner I'd hosted the night before: roast beef, Yorkshire pudding, and gravy. His wife invited me to stay for dinner. She made a chicken pot pie and heated the leftovers I brought. We ate at the dining room table as their two-year-old thrashed about in his high chair, pouring milk on himself and trying to play a rice cracker as if it were a harmonica.

There was no coffee. I was driving and, since I just got my driver's licence and can't have any alcohol in my system, I didn't have a glass of wine. There was no dessert, or music, or other guests, or an agenda. It was terrific.

Because in the end, it's about connecting with people over food. That's what's important to me. Within this book, hopefully, I've provided some guidance so that more people can make that happen more often, and with greater comfort.

ACKNOWLEDEGEMENTS

P EOPLE ARE ONLY GOING TO READ A THANK-YOU page if their name is on it. And if it is, you want a bit more meat than just being on a list. As this book has a section devoted to saying thank you, I hope you'll forgive me if I go on.

If I have left your name off this list, please do not take it personally. It's just that you've done nothing for me lately.

First I'd like to thank Lily Cho and Jesse Brown, separately. This book wouldn't exist without either of them. It was Lily who bought me that copy of Ruth Reichl's memoir, suggested I cook lunch for Reichl, and conceived of this book. Not only did Jesse name the Fed column, and not only has he been a regular cast member of my dinner parties, but he has been good-natured about accepting my public abuse.

The bad host Jesse Brown, as featured in these pages, is a fictional character, his blunders a composite of real-life dinner blunders, committed by real-life blunderers, some or all of whom may or may not be named Jesse Brown.

My many editors at the *Toronto Star* have had a massive influence on me, directly or indirectly altering the course of my life and work. Jen Bain opened the front door for me, advising me to apply for a job. Lesley Taylor (who terrorized me during a ninety-minute interview) championed the idea of hiring me. Alison Uncles supported me through my first year of professional writing, while Katie Ellis quietly taught me everything I know. She did it so unobtrusively that I wasn't even aware of being mentored. Kim Honey came up with the idea for the Fed column. We didn't really know what it was when we started. It's not like there is a long history of dinner party interview columns from which we could draw inspiration. Kim allowed it breathing room, probably resisting the urge to tinker too much, trusting that the writing would find a way to make the column function. Thank you to Janet Hurley for not firing me, making this column the longest job I've ever held. And of course to Christine Loureiro, who started at the *Star* the same time as me, a copy editor who became my boss. In a shrinking newspaper culture where writers barely get any attention, Christine made time to call me about stories, even if that had to be after 10 p.m. Though mostly she was a stopgap against me going over my monthly usage of the word penis.

Everyone should have a friend like Jen Agg, who never flinches from telling me what I'm doing wrong. When, as I refilled her glass of Riesling, she told me that my serving skills had gotten better (not good, but better), it was like getting the okay signal from Johnny Carson.

Emma Segal, the official go-with gal. She has never needed more of a pitch than "Will you come to dinner Friday?" (Unlike that lousy Jesse Brown, who wants to know what's on the menu before he says yes.)

My produce supplier, Pots, and my butcher, Peter, have helped put good food on the table.

Dr. Laura Adams (I'm certain that Laura will have finished her PhD by the time this sees print) was the one who famously, and scientifically, decreed, "Girls like napkins."

Thanks to Sandy Butts, esq., for letting me steal a line.

Kathryn Borel, for everything. If I ever got one break in this life, Kathryn gave it to me.

Now I'm getting all Sammy Maudlin, but if it weren't for Max Mandel showing me how to be a freelancer, I don't know that I would have figured out how to work from home, how to discipline myself. Mostly Max is an inspiration, for never pursuing that orchestra job.

Not only did Sarah Polley write a lovely introduction, but if it weren't for her, I would not have lost my virginity.

My unofficial helpers: Jonathan Goldsbie and Brigitte Noel. Brigitte has done fantastic work as a research assistant. If anyone at Anansi is impressed with the background material I presented, that was all Brigitte. Goldsbie, friend to many, enemy to many more, could be called the casting agent for Fed. As a dinner guest, he always knows when to talk and when to listen.

Mika Bareket talked me into teaching the class at her store, Good Egg. I think she also maybe whispered into the ear of Anansi publisher Sarah MacLachlan that this would be a neat book. And the good people of Anansi have been nothing but supportive the whole way.

Mark Medley might look like a rumpled muppet, but he is a gracious fountain of information and advice about the publishing industry, of which I knew nothing before starting this project.

I have never met Steve Murray, who illustrated these pages. But I make this promise to you, dear reader. I will hunt Mr. Murray. I will eat his flesh and destroy every record of his existence except for this book, making it a rare collector's item.

Book writing is vastly different from newspaper writing, where the facts must be at the top and there is no space for stray thoughts. Jared Bland, who I suspect had more to do with this book than I yet know, steered me through this temporal shift, coaxing me to take my time, at first with directions such as "Corey, I feel like this chapter begins a little abruptly. Could you take a go at a slightly more luxurious introductory paragraph?" By the time we got to the end it was just, "Need intro." Two of life's greatest extravagances are colleagues who take the time to explain things properly and the shorthand that develops once you understand each other.

Finally, how could I forget the people who raised me? I wouldn't be who I am today if I hadn't been taught about the difference between right and wrong and the value of hard work. So thank you, television.

COREY MINTZ hosts dinner parties in his home every week for his popular *Toronto Star* column, "Fed." Before that he was a restaurant critic. And before that he worked for a living, as a cook. In the past three years, he has hosted more than 150 dinner parties. He began without napkins or stemware, serving wine out of Nutella jars. But after hosting politicians, artists, academics, monkeys, librarians, chefs, sommeliers, cops, lawyers, psychologists, a spy, a forager, a rabbi, a gambler, a drug addict, and a mayor, he's become a pro.